Specially Educated

Specially Educated

K. Basinger, Ph.D.

Copyright © 2012 by K. Basinger

All rights reserved. This book, or parts thereof, may not be reproduced in any form without permission of the copyright owner.

Specially Educated/ K. Basinger, Ph.D.

ISBN 978-0985825904

1st Edition

All names (including the author) have been changed to protect identity.

Names, characters, and places have been changed, and any resemblance to persons, living or dead, business establishments, locales or other organizations is entirely coincidental.

To contact the author: specially_educated@hotmail.com.

Author's Note

This book is non-fiction. The story is real, the child is real and the author is real. (Even the Ex is real.) For various reasons names, places and programs have been purposely changed. There are chapters when the narrative spans across several years, followed by other chapters that span across the same years, inducing a bit of jumping back and forth in time. This is intentional (and at times perhaps confusing) because many of the interventions and expressions of parental rights were ongoing simultaneously for several years and the results of these activities could not be properly expressed in an entirely sequential manner.

Contents

Introduction i

Terms and Definitions vii

Cast of Characters xi

Part 1 – Background 1

   Bundle of Joy 3

   Early Years 6

   He Will Never Read 12

   Elementary Years 15

   The Bermuda Triangle 19

   Being Ostracized 21

   Band and the Clarinet 24

   Middle School, Lockers and Occupational Therapy 29

   The Turning Point 35

Part 2 – Interventions and Meetings 43

   The Letter Writing Begins 45

   Learning Cursive 52

   One Half of "L" 64

   Learning Measurements 66

   Learning Math 71

   The Aides 75

   Teacher Meetings 79

   Maps and Data 83

   Special Games and Activities 86

   Five IEP Meetings and an Expert 92

   The Writing Tutor 95

   NeuroPsych Returns 99

Learning a Foreign Language *102*
Learning to Write *105*
Doodling *109*
Math Reasoning *112*
Teacher Meetings – Part 2 ...... *118*
State Mandated Graduation Tests and the Waiver *120*

Part 3 – Motivating School Administrators **131**
Data, Bad Data and Useless Data *133*
Making the Chart *140*
Objective Data *149*
Subjective Data *154*
Reading Up on Case Law *158*
Complaint Strategy *164*
Layman's Interpretation of the Law *175*

Part 4 – On Toward Independence **183**
Teen Years *185*
Driving *188*
Graduation *192*
Driving – Part 2 ...... *195*

Part 5 – Reflections **201**
Never? Or A Different Way? *203*
Educating Family *206*
Educating Mom *210*
Educating the School *215*
The System Has No Memory *218*
The "High" Cost of Tutoring *220*

In Summary **227**

About the Cover

The cover contains a scan from artwork my son designed in elementary school. The picture reflects his "Love of Music" and contains swatches from a newspaper, fabric and cardboard paper interlaced with paint and ink.

There are a few samples of other artwork contained in this document, all that I found interesting, either because of the color choices or because of the visual impact. "Sunshine" precedes Part 1 and is made of painted clay. This is very cheerful and colorful and hangs on the back porch.

The drawing at the beginning of Part 2 ("Black and White") is a drawing of white chalk on black paper that my son created in elementary school. I found it to be Picasso-like.

The photo at the beginning of Part 3 is of a clay head he created. He has always maintained a fascination for the dark side and I think this is a depiction of "The Guy Down Below." Notice the two horns.

The flower painting (perhaps a Rembrandt interpretation) at the beginning of Part 4 actually is framed and hangs on my dining room wall. This is a photo of that painting. My son also created "Flowers" in elementary school and it was composed with different kinds of paint. He put a lot of focus on the spots on the primary flower. From across the room, it looks very professional.

I was never sure what the painting was at the beginning of Part 5 but I loved the colors and lines. "Sea of Flowers" has graced the family room for years.

Acknowledgements

I want to thank my mother for her hard work on some early editing of several of the first chapters. I really appreciate the additional editing and critique from Geri McClure who helped to form this document into a more readable script. And thanks to my supportive sister-in-law who helped with some of the creative aspects.

I totally appreciate all the support from Ex over the years. I may have used curse words in the vicinity of his name at times and we didn't always see eye-to-eye, but we both have always had the same goal of improving conditions for Bubba.

Big round of applause for Bubba. A totally unique individual.

And of course a big thanks to the rest of the cast of characters that all played a role in inspiring me to write down this story.

Introduction

The term `child with a disability' means a child with mental retardation, hearing impairments (including deafness), speech or language impairments, visual impairments (including blindness), serious emotional disturbance (referred to in this title as `emotional disturbance'), orthopedic impairments, autism, traumatic brain injury, other health impairments, or specific learning disabilities; and who, by reason thereof, needs special education and related services.[1]

What is special education? The government defines it as "specifically designed instruction, at no cost to the parents, to meet the unique needs of a child with a disability…"[2]

I am the recipient of a special education by virtue of being a parent of a student diagnosed as a child needing a special education. My instruction was not specifically designed – no one could have designed the process

---

[1] Individuals with Disabilities Education Improvement Act of 2004, Section 602, Definitions.

[2] Ibid.

we (Bubba, Ex and I) went through. It was not at "no cost to the parents" as there has been great cost – both in time, energy and financial resources. I have spent considerable resources getting a special education delivered to my child. The special education Bubba received eventually met his unique needs, although much of the education that met his unique needs took place at home, not in the public school. And finally, it is not clear to me, after many years in special education, that Bubba even has a disability. I am not sure that there is anything he is unable to do that other humans are able to do.

As the parent, I have been specially educated by two different public school districts, various private schools, an educational bureaucracy at the state level, educational and psychology experts, my family and the community. I have been told "he'll never," and "he can't," "he doesn't" and "he won't be able to." I have been told "we can't" and "we don't." I have had to respond "he can," "we can" and "he needs" and when the educators "will not" then "I will." I am now ready to be certified for enrollment in a mental health institution where perhaps I can take time to completely understand everything I learned. And use it for what? Unfortunately, I am not sure there is any purpose for any of what I learned, but I went ahead and logged the story, more to vent than anything else.

In the course of my special education, I have had the counsel of a couple of attorneys, several psychologists, pediatric vision specialists, pediatricians, occupational therapists, speech therapists, tutors, school district administrators, teachers, a parent advocacy group, neuropsychologists, and even religious leaders. There have been recommendations of glasses, vision therapy, occupational therapy, sensory integration therapy, medications, physical therapy, and tutoring to name a few. There have been declarations of different kinds of disabilities and declarations of no disability.

My "special" education started very innocuously. The plot progressed much like a Steven King novel, where the main character's life is very normal and predictable at the start of the book. Then there is a strange occurrence that the main character shrugs off as an anomaly. Then there may be another oddity and the reader gets clued in that there is something abnormal in the works. But the main character may not get that feeling, even though there is a dark cloud forming on the horizon and they progress through the days unaware of what the future holds.

Then all kinds of strange events and people (or non-people) join the cast and the main character wakes up one day and finds that he or she is smack in the middle of a world of weirdness.

Ex and I wandered through the first five years of Bubba's life oblivious to strange occurrences, shrugging them off as events all (or many) parents go through with their children. Oddly enough, and it sounds a bit funny, kindergarten was the year when we awoke to a world of weirdness – coincidentally the year Bubba met the public school system.

My son needed a special education; I think every child probably does. Every child is different; that is true. The special education, as delivered, would theoretically only be appropriate for one child (that is, if it worked). The public educational model is designed (I believe) to fit a typical, normal group of kids. Those who don't fit into the "normal" box are designated as needing special education or a gifted education, or sometimes both. Not fitting into the box put our family (and especially Bubba) on a painful, frustrating path.

If the special education being received by the fourteen-plus percent of children in the United States is anything like the special education bestowed upon my son by the public school system, then those kids are being cheated. If the expectations set for the fourteen-plus percent of the children are as ridiculously low as the expectations that were set for my son, then those kids are being robbed - robbed of future opportunities and sentenced to a life that falls far short of their potential. More special education kids are graduating. That sounds like a good thing, but are they proficient in math or reading? A 2008 report supported by the U.S. Office of Special Education Programs estimates the math proficiency rate of high school students with disabilities at 23%, and middle school reading proficiency at 29%. Yet the graduation rate has increased to around 80%.[3]

People have told me that my interactions with my son's school will help other children or their parents. I don't believe that. Public education, even in a small school district is a bureaucracy. Each year I found myself facing a different cast of characters. Special education directors

---

[3] "Trends in the Participation and Performance of Students with Disabilities," National Center on Educational Outcomes, *Technical Report 50*, July 2008.

came and went and different teachers were assigned each year. To think that the school district personnel pass along information requires an assumption that the system would behave like a caring human being, and it doesn't. The system has a very short memory and some parts of the system are not aware of the actions and decisions made in another part of the system, even in a small bureaucracy. So thinking that some other family interacting with the public school systems we interacted with will benefit from my experience is giving too much credence to the system.

I was assured by a parent advocate that "no one knows your son better than you do." I think that is true. But even if I were a licensed neuropsychologist, *and* a medical doctor, *and* perhaps a teacher as well, I would still be a parent and therefore not an expert in a special education team meeting. I would be a biased parent. So I may spend years raising and teaching my own child, be the holder of the most complete history and data on the child, but will still be a secondary member of the team that makes decisions regarding my child's education. Because in the eyes of the law, the education agency is presumed to be correct in their determinations of needed services, unless the parents can prove otherwise. And, to prove otherwise, the parents will need to provide experts and data that support their contention.

So, I am left with scars of what has seemed at times to be a life or death fight. Ex was reduced to a non-participant on Bubba's education team, his ideas waved off because he is Bubba's father? Or the other biased parent? And while Bubba looks perfectly normal on the outside, what scars are on the inside?

And in spite of the frustration, the pain, and the inherent flaws in the system, we pushed forward. Pushed Bubba and pushed ourselves so that he was not one of the 70 or 80 percent of special education kids that are not proficient. He easily could have been, yet "he does" and "he can." The phrase "he'll never" was clearly wrong.

I use Bubba to represent my son in this writing and of course that is not his real name. Ex is his father, and that is not his name either. I refer to "The Program" which was the program we used outside the public school system to improve Bubba's core academic skills in reading, writing and math.

Specially Educated

The narrative in this book takes place over the first eighteen years of Bubba's life. I have been told that the writing improves as the book progresses. Indeed, the graphs with their V-shapes shown in the book reflect more than reading, writing and math scores. They also reflect Bubba's confidence as a learner and my confidence as his mother.

I don't present many recommendations in this book; this is a true story and I don't feel qualified to advise other parents. I have been told that I write with an odd sense of humor and my perceptions and feelings about many of the events described in this book have evolved over time. But of all the concepts, terms, and feelings I uncovered along the way there was no more important activity than to keep written records, because if it wasn't written down, ***it didn't happen.***

Terms and Definitions

I am including some terms and definitions in this section that are used later in the book. The definitions are generally my interpretations of their meanings.

IDEA – the *Individuals with Disabilities Education Act*, the special education law.[4] This law defines special education terms, requirements and responsibilities of the public special education system. This law originated from the *Education for All Handicapped Children Act* that was enacted in 1975. The intent of these acts is to protect the rights of children with disabilities and their families.

Learning Disability – The term is used interchangeably with learning disorder in some places. A specific learning disability according to *IDEA* means "a disorder in 1 or more of the basic psychological processes involved in understanding or in using language, spoken or written, which disorder may manifest itself in the imperfect ability to listen, think, speak, read, write, spell, or do mathematical calculations."[5]

---

[4] A complete description of *IDEA* and the entire document can be found at www.ed.gov.

[5] U.S. Code, Title 20, Chapter 33, Subchapter 1, Section 1401, Definitions.

IEP – Individualized Education Program. According to *IDEA*, this means "a written statement for each child with a disability that is developed, reviewed and revised in accordance with Section 614(d)." Section 614(d) describes the evaluations, eligibility determinations, IEPs, and educational placements in *Title 1 – Amendments to IDEA*.

Neuropsychologist – The school psychologists that we encountered generally held masters degrees and were trained in psychology. For a student evaluation, they would spend a couple hours performing IQ tests and achievement tests and then present their results to the IEP team. A neuropsychologist has a PhD and is trained in both neurology and psychology and how the two interact. The neuropsychologist focuses on brain functioning, performs a much broader array of tests (ours took three days) and recommends activities specific to their analysis of the test subject (child).

IQ Testing and IQ Split – IQ testing is used to measure intelligence. It has two major components – verbal and performance. The verbal component involves language mastery and the performance component involves patterns, logic and puzzle manipulation. Each of those two components has subparts that are rolled into two averages. The two components are combined or averaged to get the full scale IQ score. People can favor one component or the other. A difference of over 10 points between the verbal and performance scores was identified as significant by Bubba's neuropsychologist.

Pragmatic Language – The neuropsychologist called pragmatic language the ability to use and understand social language. He mentioned that Bubba had difficulty reading non-verbal cues, such as knowing when to speak and when to cut it short. I understood it as a general sense of the rules of social communication.

Verbal Learner – I describe Bubba as a verbal learner. He learns more efficiently through words than pictures. Many times, graphs, pictures, and diagrams generated confusion instead of clarity. This is related to the term visual-spatial disorder, or problems with comprehension of visual input and how visual objects relate to each other. This can also be interpreted as how parts of objects make up a whole object.

Convergence Insufficiency – This refers to the ability of the two eyes to work together to focus on objects. Vision therapy and prism glasses were two techniques recommended by our pediatric optometrists to improve Bubba's vision.

The Red Neck - The "red neck" is a symptom I have experienced and have seen experienced by several different characters in public school administration. It is a physical flushing red of the neck that appeared to occur when a person was either frustrated or caught with their "pants down," as they say.

Cast of Characters

That was the moment, I think – then, just at that moment – when I felt something cold and blue inside me. There was a moment – just then – when I felt like slugging Arnie and dragging him away. Something came into the old man's eyes. Not just the gleam; it was something behind the gleam.[6]

This book is perhaps a long essay of events, actions and inactions, my own personal feelings about certain experiences, interspersed with facts that tell a sort of happy, sad story about my interactions and my perceptions of Bubba's primary school years. At times, I was Arnie, turning into the old man with a gleam of near-insanity as I struggled to make sense of situations that I had never imagined encountering. I became obsessed with trying to make things normal, while carrying on a professional life in a field where root causes of problems were eventually ferreted out and solved rationally using logical, best practices with testing and results. I struggled to deal with an educational system and people that operated on an entirely different model of relying on sketchy data, untested approaches and little accountability.

The main characters in this book are me (of course), Bubba (my young one) and Bubba's father (Ex). I recruited NeuroPsych when Bubba was entering seventh grade and this man was able to validate a large part of

---

[6] Stephen King, *Christine* (New York: The Viking Press, 1983), 9.

my experience, forging the way for targeted progress. The list of coordinators represents the hand-off of responsibility from one administrator to the next, setting the stage for incredible frustration on my part as I spent session after session re-explaining what was, what wasn't, what happened and what didn't, over and over again.

Bubba – This is the angelic child I brought into this world. He can do nothing wrong, of course. Fortunately Bubba has a sense of humor and a deep-rooted understanding of what is right and what is wrong. He will avoid trying new things or doing things for himself if he can get away with it. He is now tall and blond and can carry me around the living room.

The Author – Overprotective, overeducated Mama Bear who desperately sought to maintain a sense of humor. I am a tall, athletic, red-head who can get obsessed with issues from time to time. I believe in thinking outside the box and trying different methods for teaching. I have spent most of my working career immersed in data. I have been known to be emotional, have cried at a mediation with the school district, yelled at an administrator "YES or NO, WHICH IS IT?" and have taken up studying *Judge Judy* to get a proper perspective.

Ex – This is Bubba's father, a relatively fit, slightly over-educated, civil engineer who also has a professional engineering license. He has dark, black hair and darkish skin and is known to have conversations with himself in the mirror that often contain the expression "Motherf***er," especially after meeting with school district officials and administration. Ex is a young 50-something who never got the "red neck" at meetings, although he would curse in the school parking lot afterwards. He walks with a bit of a swagger. (After school meetings the swagger was more related to physical pain.) Ex hung in there for years at meetings with district folks even though they ignored most of what he said. He finally got frustrated, ill and suggested that I "take care of it."

NeuroPsych – This fellow was a PhD-level neuropsychologist who did his dissertation on Non-Verbal Learning Disorder, a category of kids with visual-spatial, social and fine motor issues. He was a tall, good-looking fellow, probably in his late thirties. He was fit and trim and liked to use the word "kiddo" to describe his patients. NeuroPsych was on a first name basis with most of the school district folks because he also had a contract to provide services to the school. This turned out to be a two-edged sword because he knew the system, but he tended to be somewhat reserved and politically correct in the team meetings. He never turned red, cried or yelled out "You Idiots!" like I wished he would. He did, however, tell me in private that what was happening at the school with Bubba was a tragedy. He was well respected around the city and state where we live.

District Coordinator 1 – This was a woman who worked for the large, urban public school district where Bubba attended kindergarten and first grade. She wasn't too happy when I contacted the State Department of Education to obtain an independent evaluation of Bubba. In the spirit of the military, she kept a short, cropped hairstyle and had a set of constantly pursed lips. She was short, but carried a big stick and rarely developed the "red neck." She had her hands full dealing with one of the largest urban school districts in the state.

District Coordinator 2 – This was a woman who was around 55 to 60 years old. She rarely had a smile on her face. She generally didn't demonstrate the "red neck" in my presence that so many of the other special education folks exhibited. Her hair was a brownish-grey mix; she carried a few extra pounds and was not much of a snazzy dresser. She was the coordinator of the small, suburban district we moved to at the end of first grade and had been the coordinator there for years. She maintained her position as the district grew while the supporting village converted itself from a small, non-descript area to an affluent Stepford-like community.

District Coordinator 3 – This woman also worked for the affluent, small, suburban school district. She replaced Number 2 when Number 2 retired to go play golf at the end of Bubba's seventh grade year. Number 3 was a victim of the "red neck" constantly in my presence and was often seen with a shocked expression on her face, reflecting her consistent responses of "What? You want special services for your child? We can't do that." Although this woman was the coordinator, her title was consultant and she may not have been a district employee. I could never figure out this arrangement – blame deflection perhaps? This was the woman (and she was another middle-aged lady, albeit a better dresser than Number 2) who didn't understand the bell curve, a commonly used function for communicating student performance and comparing performance to what is typical or "normal." Her lack of understanding was a real learning disability for someone in charge of relaying testing results to parents.

High School Coordinator – This was the only male I encountered in a school district administrative role during Bubba's school years. This fellow actually read the report that NeuroPsych had written up for the school district because I saw him browsing it during the one team meeting that he attended. Okay, maybe he didn't actually read it. He was probably around sixty and had retired once, but was asked to return to the district. So he may have been a double-dipper, receiving his pension and a salary as well. He did look pretty happy all the time! He was a sensible fellow who proclaimed "if you find something that works, stick with it." This was a man after my own heart. We never saw him again after that one meeting, unfortunately. He changed his title and became responsible for some other aspect of the education system.

District Coordinator 4 – This woman was about my age (in her late forties, but looking much younger) with long reddish-brown hair and a small, very pretty face. She was a middle school coordinator when we first met (her first day on the job landed her smack in our first mediation) who eventually rose to the top when Number 3 (the consultant) retired to go work on her lake home. Number 4 and I were not averse to actually yelling at each other occasionally in the manner of a cat-fight that tended to provoke disturbed expressions on the other team members' faces during IEP meetings. Eventually the district's assistant superintendent stepped in to deal with me.

Assistant District Superintendent – I am making the title up because I never quite understood her real title (Director of Teaching and Learning), or what it meant. She was able to authorize checks for repayment of the neuropsychologist's services and for tutoring costs, so I eventually began dealing with the right person – the person with financial authority. This was another woman in her early fifties, with a generally calm demeanor, fashionable yet sensible work suits and short, stylish, light brown hair. She received her doctorate in education one quarter before I received mine in engineering. (She may have obtained hers first but I think mine was harder.) She didn't originally get the "red neck," but developed it later when she realized I wasn't going away. The "red neck" occurred shortly after I launched my second complaint in conjunction with her statement, "I thought we already dealt with you."

There were a variety of other characters that I encountered over the years, and I am not highlighting them here even though many of them did leave an impression. I remember every teacher that Bubba had, and there were some very good ones. There were teachers who really cared and over time began to understand the nature of the challenge in terms of Bubba's learning style. There were teachers with a good dose of common sense, and teachers who appeared more interested in their fingernails and their hair.

There were school psychologists that didn't have a prayer of understanding Bubba, but were asked to evaluate him. And there was an entire support system of friends and family who each had their own interpretation of the events, interactions, actions and inactions.

"Sunshine"

Part 1 – Background

This section describes our experiences with Bubba from the first days up through middle school. Life seemed to be a mix of normal and abnormal events and until the collision of Bubba and the school system, there wasn't a lot of confusion in my thinking. As Bubba's schooling progressed, Ex and I were confronted with a series of conflicting information that eventually led me to get serious about researching special needs children, and contacting an outside professional.

Bundle of Joy

Those who expect their babies to arrive as round and smooth and pink as a Botticelli cherub may be in for a shock.[7]

The day I went into labor was not the day I gave birth. Ex and I were hanging around the house on a warm, humid evening in June. My parents had just left, after spending the weekend at our house in hopes of labor. I was unable to deliver on those hopes. Sunday afternoon Mom, Dad, Ex and I had our butts parked on various couches and chairs in the living room, staring at each other without much to say. Thank goodness there wasn't a grandfather clock in the room. Finally, after an hour or so of awkward silence, Mom and Dad decided to head to the north to go back home, disappointed I am sure.

About two hours later, I started getting some aches in the lower abdomen, followed by some periodic stronger pains. Ex began yelling and pacing around the bedroom frantically. "We have to go to the hospital!" he proclaimed.

---

[7] Arlene Eisenberg, Heidi E. Murkoff, and Sandee E. Hathaway, B.S.N., *What to Expect When You're Expecting* (New York: Workman Publishing Company, 1991).

"Oh. I think it's still early," I said, clueless.

"No, we have to go. Now!" His panic level was creeping upward. After an hour or so of this exchange, I finally relented. I must have had a bag packed, or packed a bag of supplies, but I honestly don't remember.

Ex and I hauled it into the car and headed to the hospital, about a thirty minute drive. The freeway bumps reverberated through the car, through my body, and I yelled at him to slow down. But he was in a hurry. When we got to the hospital, the staff debated whether or not to send us back home because it was a little too early. The dilation was minimal. I had only just begun. Eventually, they decided that we should go ahead and check into the hospital. I found my room, complete with rocking chair, bed and bathroom. It was very nice for a temporary layover.

Labor went on throughout the night. We walked, tried to sleep, and rocked in the big rocking chair. The night was a blur. The next morning I was finally able to reach my parents and they headed back south from their home, hoping to get to the hospital in time. It was a two-hour drive at least.

They needn't have worried and they arrived in plenty of time. The day wore on and around noon I was taken to surgery because Bubba's heart rate had dropped. Once I was put on my side (to place the epidural), his heart rate recovered so the doctor sent me back to my room to wait some more. I spent the next six or seven hours lying on one side and then the other, still waiting.

Finally, the doctor lost patience, I had lost patience, and we agreed on proceeding with a cesarean section. It couldn't have been twenty minutes later, and voila, baby. Mom and Ex were in the delivery room with me. Ex was standing next to me, trying to be supportive, holding my hand and saying "Breathe."

I couldn't see my mother because there was a cloth draped between my upper and lower torso, but she actually captured the event with her camera. She was clicking away on the other side of the white curtain where all the nurses and the doctor were standing. She has more stomach than I do, but I have a set of interesting pictures as a result.

"He's a nine!" the doctor exclaimed. I was happy to see all ten fingers and ten toes on the little guy. "No, he's a ten!" Handing me my bundle of joy, the doctor leaned in closer and added, "I rarely give a baby a ten."

Wow, I thought. A ten. And ten fingers and ten toes. And a kick-ass set of lungs. He was blond and cute even though his nose was all wrinkled up. He must have been really smashed up in there.

But he was beautiful. A little blond fuzz for hair, perfect skin, really good lungs, and I mean really good lungs. Chunky little legs and strong. Wow again! My bundle of joy.

Early Years

> *A convulsion is a frightening thing to see in a child, but in most cases it is not dangerous in itself. In most convulsions, the child loses consciousness, the eyes roll up, the teeth are clenched, and the body or parts of the body are shaken by twitching movements.*[8]

"He's just mad," the pediatrician told me. I wanted to know why Bubba would stiffen, arch and stop breathing if we picked him up after he fell. At around the age of two we had ceased picking him up after a fall, because he would have such a strange reaction.

I remember clearly, a day when my girlfriend was visiting our home. Bubba had climbed up on a kitchen chair at the table close to where we were chatting. He slipped off the chair and banged his head on the chair back. My girlfriend (a mother and a grandmother) rushed to Bubba who was crying. I stood back because I had become intimidated by his reactions at this point. She lifted him up and his back arched while his entire body stiffened. Her face flushed red as she held him out to me with a panic stricken look in her eyes. I didn't know what to tell her and I mumbled, "We usually don't pick him up if he falls."

---

[8] Benjamin Spock M.D. and Michael B. Rothenberg, *Dr. Spock's Baby and Child Care. Sixth Edition* (New York: Simon & Schuster, 1992).

Around the same time, when Bubba was around eighteen months old, I had stayed home from work with him as he was very sick, fighting a flu-like illness. His temperature would spike and one morning I had him in the bathroom sponging him off with a cool cloth to try to bring his temperature down. He began to shake, arched backwards and ceased breathing. I immediately called 911 and the emergency squad arrived very quickly. As they transported us both to the emergency room, the technician commented that I was in no shape to drive. I admit, I'm a bit of a wimp.

Bubba was diagnosed with febrile seizures. "Febrile seizures don't cause any permanent harm," I was told by the pediatrician, after spending the day with Bubba in the emergency room. He had been running a temperature of 106 degrees for hours, even after having different fever reducers, and after having been on antibiotics for several days. The doctors in the emergency room were not able to determine what caused the fever and ordered several tests to try to isolate the cause, including meningitis testing using a spinal tap. Finally, after intravenous injections of antibiotics his fever came down and we were able to return home that evening.

When we went to the pediatrician's office the next week, Bubba was feeling better. "We'll put him on antibiotics for a few months to keep him from getting the high temperatures with any bad infections he gets in the future," the doctor told us. This had been his second high-fever seizure episode.

Experiencing those events put a deep-seated fear in my mind and heart whenever there was the beginning of a cold, a slight fever or a fall. I really didn't like the emergency room scene and this may have been the root of becoming a true Mama Bear. Most of the seizures and breath-holding episodes happened during the year after Bubba turned one and tapered off by the time he was three.

But then when he was around three, he began to stutter severely and he eventually stopped speaking. For about a month he rarely spoke, but as time went on he began dragging out the first syllable of each sentence and eventually got the confidence to talk again. Over time he lost the drag, although occasionally (even now) he used long pauses between thoughts or sometimes right in the middle of an explanation to get his words out. Then people began finishing his sentences for him, including me.

Silly me. I didn't think this was entirely normal, but I certainly didn't see anything to be too worried about. Ex and I took Bubba to be tested at the speech and hearing clinic, just to get an outsider's opinion. The speech and hearing clinician didn't seem too concerned, telling us not to dwell on it and let it run its course. What was normal anyway?

Okay, when he drew pictures, his drawings looked odd. We had a big, portable chalkboard his grandmother gave him and he loved to draw on the board. His drawings were mostly lines slashing though each other, and he usually finished with scribbles covering up the drawing. Not an artist? Maybe later.

And tying shoes was a pretty big deal. We worked on that for years and years with a lot of frustration. Even at fifteen, he just left his shoes tied and slid in and out of them. Not that big of a deal to me, because I wear loafers. I thought this was evidence of some fine motor problems for Bubba, but I was content with his workaround.

But this kid was sitting up at six months, and walking at twelve months and talking shortly after. He rolled when he was supposed to and smiled, and pointed and used a fork to smash his spaghetti all over his face, just like he was supposed to. It really wasn't until the frequent vaccinations, colds, fevers, ear infections and seizures that he became slightly more subdued. But not anything really abnormal, I thought.

The stuttering probably worried me the most, especially when he quit talking, and I can remember Ex frequently expressing worry. It was unusual for Ex to become concerned about much and it broke our hearts to hear Bubba struggle. But we stayed patient and Bubba seemed to work himself out of that problem over time.

None the less, Bubba was a very happy boy. He liked games and toys that all kids like. He climbed up and down the stairs, played on the neighbor's trampoline, mastering the front flip. He put together a pretty impressive monkey bar routine – very smooth. He was solidly left-handed and could accurately bean me with a ball from across the room.

The seizures, breath-holding and stuttering marked the extent of the oddities, and for every day when there was an upsetting occurrence, there were another hundred days that were perfectly normal. Normal, right?

He learned the alphabet early and then all his numbers. I even thought he was reading early until I figured out he had every story memorized after I read it to him once. Nothing too odd, right?

Bubba spent his days at the sitter's house because both Ex and I worked during the day. There were four or five other kids at her house (usually all boys) that were about his age. Ex or I would pick him up each day and find a happy, engaged boy. The sitter, who was a kind, quiet, middle-aged woman told me once, "Bubba will learn things in his own time, in his own way." Boy did that turn out to be true. But all-in-all, we had a smart, athletic, happy fellow when he started kindergarten.

During kindergarten, the school district wanted to evaluate Bubba for a learning disability. They felt that he was having problems in the classroom and so Ex and I agreed to the evaluation. I was totally shocked during a one-on-one with the school district's psychologist when she informed me that Bubba would never read, write or be an athlete, and that he was mildly mentally retarded. And she also informed me that he was right-handed.

I questioned the report, noting that they had done the evaluation the week after Bubba had fallen off the monkey bars and broken his left arm. She tersely replied, "That won't make any difference."

"But he was in pain and not sleeping," I pleaded. "And he is not right-handed, he's left-handed," I added.

"No he's not."

"Yes he is."

"No he's not. His teacher told me so."

"I am his mother and I am quite sure he is left-handed." I was getting really angry at this point. I stared at the psychologist, dumbfounded.

As I continued to question the accuracy of the report, I ran into my first set of road blocks. I requested an independent evaluation and was ignored by the school district. So I called the State Department of Education where I conversed with a sympathetic advisor. After I explained the circumstances and what I was told by the school psychologist, he told me he would help get Bubba an independent evaluation. I remember him telling me of his early education where he was taught to write upside-down. This was memorable and upsetting to him and he informed me that he was also a lefty. He felt that lefties had their own unique challenges to learning in a right-handed world. This fellow must have thrown a grenade into the public school district administration offices because that same day (after weeks of being unable to get a call returned) I received a call from the District Coordinator 1.

"How dare you go around the chain of command!" These were the first words out of her mouth. Imagine.

"I don't know what your chain of command is," I puffed back. "I want an independent evaluation for Bubba at the Children's Hospital by a qualified psychologist."

Bubba was able to get an independent evaluation and it was at no cost to us, the parents. The independent evaluator declared that there were some deficits, but that she felt he did not have a learning disability. So I had two reports that seemed to reflect two different kids. Perfectly normal, right?

Unfortunately, by the end of kindergarten, Bubba would no longer even pick up a pen or pencil to write – the only way he would write was if I would let him tell a story and I would put the pencil to paper. I struggled to find out what was not working for him in the school setting because it seemed that he was getting unhappier by the day.

He had already been stabbed in the hand by a young girl with a pencil during class, and stabbed by another with a paper clip. Not exactly weapons of mass destruction, but I was beginning to fear for his safety.

In first grade, I began visiting the school; I watched the typical school day and was dismayed. Kids came in a half-hour late, wandered in and out of the classroom and the teacher spent most of her time attempting hands-off discipline. Bubba had an unhappy look on his face, which was fairly typical of the kids at that school, especially as they moved into later grades.

The teacher had Bubba using some strange podium that was supposed to help him write. Even this was ineffective as it was set up on his right side for a right-hander and he had to reach across his body in an awkward position to put pencil to paper. They apparently still didn't recognize he was left-handed. I clearly remember looking at Bubba as I was visiting one day in first grade and the look on his face, near tears, all but crying "Get me out of here!"

Bubba's kindergarten year and first grade year were life-changing for all of us. He had been given a sentence by the school administration that cast a shadow of doubt on the possibilities for his future. That marked the end of the early years and the beginning of a long road to understanding the law, learning difficulties or differences, school districts and some of the less attractive characteristics of my fellow human beings. It also marked the end of our stint in that particular school district.

He Will Never Read

How Can the Child with Autism Be Taught to Read?
- *Make Reading an Enjoyable Activity by Using Authentic High Interest Visual Materials,*
- *Use a Phonetic Approach,*
- *Use Relevant Context Clues, Social Stories and Comic Strip Sequences*[9]

What a marvel my little bundle of joy turned out to be. At the age of four he could read books already! That's what I thought, but what I thought wasn't true. There was actually some kind of super-powered, mega-ram, mega-watt, mega-memory power in Bubba. One pass through a book when Mom read it and the next time Bubba could "read" it.

Imagine how perplexed I was that day when the school psychologist told me that he would never read. That proclamation didn't bode well for Bubba's future – indeed what exactly were the possibilities for him if he couldn't even read? And what was it about Bubba that made it seem to the school district that he would never be capable of reading?

---

[9] James S. Vacca, "Autistic Children Can Be Taught to Read," *International Journal of Special Education*. 22 (3), 2007.

Specially Educated

It's not clear to me how I came into possession of the book entitled *Why Johnny Can't Read*.[10] I suppose that at some point in my research on how to fix the "never will read" problem, I came across the radical ravings of the author, Rudolf Flesch.

I also acquired a game set called "The Phonics Game Starter Kit" that I had heard about (probably on a television commercial).[11] There seemed to be two schools of thought on learning how to read – one was phonics based and the other was the "word method" that used memorization of words and would over time allow the child to read.

I had learned how to read using the phonics method, or sounding out the words. The sounds had to be learned and then the associated groups of sounds were learned. After reading about Johnny, I was further convinced that phonics was the way to go for Bubba, also.

The last section of that book contains a sequential list of letters and then phonic combinations and practice pages. The pages move from simple short vowel words to long vowels and then onto consonant and vowel combinations. Letter sounds are listed first, of course.

Around the middle of first grade, each night Bubba and I would lie on the bed mastering a page or reviewing a page. Progress was immediate, and after a month or so he was able to read single syllable words (at least I think he was reading them). Some nights we would play a round of phonics using the game, but mostly we stuck to the back of the book.

In two months, he had mastered the complex phonic combinations. By three months, we had finished practicing all 70 (or so) pages in the back of the book, spending about fifteen minutes a day, most days of the week. We stopped when there were no more pages to read, the game was getting boring and Bubba really could read very well. He especially liked action books with good and evil characters, and I made him read books to me that I hadn't previously read to him, just to be sure.

---

[10] Rudolf Flesch, *Why Johnny Can't Read: And What You Can Do About It* (Harper & Row Publishers, Inc., 1955).

[11] "The Phonics Game Starter Kit™", Published by A Better Way of Learning, 1994.

The experience of meeting with the psychologist, and being told "never," combined with several visits to the school led to a desire to relocate to another school district, or find a private school. As I searched for a better district, I checked for schools that demonstrated usage of the phonics method for reading because I saw the progress he made using that method. I looked for a place where Bubba would be safe. I looked for a school district where he wouldn't get stabbed. I searched for a place where kids smiled and behaved, and where the teacher had an organized, clutter free classroom. I looked for a district that was smaller, that contained, hopefully, a more caring staff and I eventually found one.

There was not a good alternative to public school as every private school we interviewed did not want to enroll Bubba. So we packed up, sold the house, and moved to the smaller, suburban, public school district.

Bubba began second grade in a new school, in a smaller, safer district, that taught reading using a phonics method. And when they tested Bubba's basic reading skills in second grade, he tested above grade level. Never, what?

Elementary Years

Something was wrong, something was out of place, out of joint. There was a chill, and not all the bright October sunshine spilling through all the high school windows in the world would dispel it. Things were as they always had been, but they were getting ready to change – I felt it.[12]

By the beginning of second grade, we found ourselves in a new school district in a new house complete with new neighbors. Bubba was happier at his new school and smiled in the mornings. I could walk him to the bus stop and almost breathe, knowing he would at least be safer in his new school. They taught reading with phonics and maintained a clean, well-disciplined classroom environment.

He was placed in the general education classroom for most classes, but was sent to the resource room for writing and math. The resource room can also be referred to as a self-contained room where only children designated as needing special education are present. The resource room teacher spent second through fifth grades teaching money (coin values), time, and had Bubba work with an occupational therapist on handwriting, as his printing was not too legible.

---

[12] Stephen King, *Christine* (New York: The Viking Press, 1983), 175.

Ex and I tried to keep Bubba engaged outside the classroom. There was Tai Kwon Do, where Bubba made it to blue belt. By third grade, he was able to play little league football, baseball and basketball. He wasn't the best athlete, but he did look good in a football uniform. Football was a big sport for both my family and Ex's family, and we encouraged him to play. He said he liked the game days with all the excitement, but began to dislike the football practices around the third year of playing. Indeed, he began crying and getting up during the night worrying about having to go to practice. It was then that I asked him to choose another sport, because I thought it was important for him to be involved in a sport for the exercise and opportunity to socialize with other students outside the classroom.

After the traumatic start in kindergarten and first grade, Bubba started having trouble getting to sleep. Either Ex or I would stay with him until he fell asleep, and then leave the room. We usually read to him, as it seemed to calm him down. The reading at night continued through middle school, and even into high school. One thing did change in high school when sometimes Bubba would read me to sleep! Ah, but I have skipped ahead.

I have read that many parents of kids like Bubba end up putting them on antidepressants or sleeping medications, or other medications that are used for attention deficit or anxiety. I had people, such as teachers, suggest he take medications. Oddly enough, his pediatrician never recommended medications, which was fine with me, because I didn't want him on any medications. Nothing stronger than fish oil, a multi-vitamin and a good book was needed for my Bubba.

In fourth grade, the folks at the new school performed Bubba's multi-factored evaluation. This is required at least once every three years by *IDEA*, and is used to determine in what areas (academically, behaviorally, functionally) the student needs special education services. The school district performed achievement tests, IQ testing and classroom observations and put the information into a written report.

After the multi-factored evaluation is performed, there is a team meeting to discuss the report and any implications for changes to the special education program. Attending this meeting was District Coordinator 2, Bubba's resource room teacher, the psychologist, Ex and I. The director informed us at the team meeting that Bubba had a specific learning disability.

"What specific learning disability is it?" I asked. I was being serious but it seemed that I had asked a stupid question. I had been given about two minutes to read the report, after which I began receiving the "looks."

"It is a specific learning disability," District Coordinator 2 answered.

"Which one, specifically?" I tried a slightly different approach.

"It's non-specific," she answered. (I would like to remind you this is a true story.)

"A non-specific, specific learning disability?" I was coming off like an asshole (or else someone was) but I couldn't help myself.

"Yes," she replied. Now I had read up on the specific learning disability (SLD) in the literature. The SLD designation was indicated when a child was not achieving according to their measured potential.

"I thought a specific learning disability was when a student's achievement scores were not as high as their IQ scores. Bubba is achieving beyond his potential, according to this report, and that would be the opposite of a specific learning disability."

A hush came over the room. I really was not trying to be an asshole – I just didn't understand, and I thought it was important to characterize the "disability" correctly. How else could we develop a proper learning program?

"Okay. He has a cognitive disability." District Coordinator 2 looked to the school psychologist, who nodded.

"What's that?" Ex asked.

"That means he has problems with his thinking processes," District Coordinator 2 responded. "We also would like to have him move to the resource room for his reading, as the reading and writing go together, and it is difficult to schedule his writing in the resource room and his reading outside the resource room."

Now, looking back, armed with all the valuable lessons I have learned, I don't think I would have caved so quickly on the request. Because what the district was doing was changing Bubba's placement for reading into a more restrictive environment, even though he was demonstrating above grade level reading skills. They were suggesting the move because it made it more convenient for their scheduling (a recurring theme as the years went by, and in direct conflict with the intent of the law). Not only that, I had the sinking feeling that there was something else not right, but couldn't really identify it at that time. I tended to be very slow to understand the implications of decisions throughout Bubba's education, primarily because I didn't always understand what Bubba's rights were and what the consequences of our decisions would be. I also felt, at that time, that I needed to make decisions immediately during the meeting and could not take the information home and read it carefully.

I had two conflicting prior reports and now a third report that seemed consistent with the report performed by the previous school district's psychologist. And now they were tagging Bubba with a different disability because he was specifically, non-specific and I was left with an inadequate explanation by the new district's staff of what his learning disability was, specifically.

Regardless, we signed off on the evaluation with a nagging sense of confusion and uneasiness. But we trusted the school district personnel and knew we were not in that horrible, large urban district anymore, and we were somewhat certain that Bubba was in better hands with this group. Looking back, it was naïve or laziness on my part or a fear of further confrontation that led me to back off when I still had unanswered questions and answers that didn't completely make sense. I also had a private evaluation from the Children's Hospital that listed a finding of no learning disability. So which was it? What was the right approach?

By fourth grade, we had heard "never read, write or be an athlete," saw above grade level reading, heard mentally retarded or non-specific specific learning disability, saw offensive lineman and home-run hitter, heard cognitive disability, and heard no learning disability. Add in witnessing Bubba's extreme dislike of writing along with the passage of fourth grade writing and reading proficiencies. Maybe it's no wonder I was confused!

The Bermuda Triangle

> *Many people are not familiar with how exotic the area is. There is no other place in the world full of so many natural mysteries...apart from its greatest mystery of unexplained disappearances.*[13]

The zone between school, the book bag and home was frequently a Bermuda Triangle. Assignments had a way of disappearing and communication, even with email technology somehow fell into mysterious, black holes.

I recently saw a brief skit on a sit-com where the mother of an exotic child experienced flashbacks of complex elementary school projects that were disclosed to her at the last minute by her son. The projects were always due the next day when there were few instructions, a lack of materials and a clear lack of appropriate time and planning. The same expression of panic was on her face that I felt so many times. Alas, I must not be alone!

Binders stuffed with papers. Spending an hour rummaging through papers each night to find an assignment that was overdue or due the next day. Why did elementary school children need so many papers anyway?

---

[13] "Exotic Waters: Take a Fantastic Journey Through the Triangle with Bruce Gernon," www.bermuda-triangle.org.

I don't think I carried a book bag to school, not even in high school, and certainly not in elementary school. And Bubba's bag wasn't filled with just a few items; it was stuffed to the gills and the zipper was bursting.

One evening, as I waited at home for the arrival of my long-time girlfriend who was visiting from San Francisco, I picked up the suburban newspaper to read. These newspapers were casually tossed in the driveway Wednesday evenings and contained stories of local interest sponsored by local advertisers. When I looked at the front page there was a large photo of a girl in Bubba's third grade class dropping an egg off the second floor balcony at the elementary school. I read the photo caption that described the science experiment and how each student had designed a protective device to, hopefully, shield the egg from cracking when it landed on the floor.

"Bubba," I said. "Look. Janie is on the front page dropping an egg."

"Hmm."

"Isn't Janie in your class?"

"Yes."

"Why didn't you have to do an egg project?" I asked.

"Mrs. Smith said if I bring it in tomorrow I can still get credit," he replied.

Needless to say, when my girlfriend arrived, the three of us spent the evening rapidly constructing an egg drop protective device, following a jumble of partially remembered instructions from Bubba. The paper based instructions were probably jammed in the book bag somewhere and forgotten.

Being Ostracized

> *Social exclusion refers to not being included within a given social network (but not necessarily ignored). Rejection is usually an explicit verbal or physical action that declares that the individual is not wanted as a member within a relationship or group.*[14]

Just like the entire special education evolved in a manner consistent with a creepy Steven King novel, so did the ostracizing process. Before Bubba entered school, he frequently played in several different "circles" of friends. There was our group of similarly aged boys whose parents all shared the same sitter. The boys played with each other while the parents worked, and in addition, we frequently had get-togethers for birthdays and special occasions as well. There were occasional sleepovers and the other usual "play dates."

Bubba also spent considerable play time with the neighbor girl who was the same age. She practically lived with her grandparents who were our next-door neighbors. Bubba was always climbing over the fence to play on their slide or trampoline, or to just have squirt gun battles. Indeed, when she took off on her bicycle without training wheels, that event was

---

[14] Kipling D. Williams, Joseph P. Forgas, William Von Hippel, *The Social Outcast: Ostracism, Social Exclusion, Rejection, and Bullying (Sydney Symposium in Social Psychology)*, (London: Psychology Press, 2005).

sufficient incentive for Bubba to do the same. And over the other fence was an ornery little fellow who was also Bubba's age who spent a lot of time playing at our house.

When we moved to our new home, it was located on a beautiful suburban street that I affectionately referred to as "Stepford." There were three or four homes within view that housed boys who were Bubba's age. Soon, he began heading up or down the street after school to play with one group or another.

Around fourth grade, things began to change. Bubba would come home from school in a not-so-special mood. I would ask him if he was going to play with "Jason" down the street. "Grunt" would be a typical reply, or "I don't want to; I may go down later." By fifth grade there was no playing with the boys on the other end of the street. When we took walks around the neighborhood and would pass one of his former "friends" there were just glaring stares. I could never get any response or information from Bubba as to what happened. But clearly, something happened and these boys didn't want to play with him anymore.

By sixth grade there were no friends or kids to hang out within our neighborhood. However, one boy around the corner, a bit of an overactive young lad, began showing up at our house. Bubba had met him at the bus stop in the morning before school and they seemed to hit it off. I was warned by another neighbor that this boy was trouble, and I had full awareness of this (imagine looking out your front window and seeing this same 11-year-old with his pants down watering the front yard – naturally!) but by this point could not fathom cutting Bubba off from the one friend he had. I let "Trouble" come in the house if he was with his sister and put him on the three-strike system. It didn't take long for him to straighten up, because I didn't hesitate to send him home if he hadn't listened by the third warning.

Not only was there an evaporation of friends, the ostracizing started to spread through the family. When your child is not welcome on teams and is not a part of teen hang-out events, it starts separating the parents from other parents as well.

By this time, most days Bubba sat alone at lunch time at school and attempts to get the school to help him integrate produced no results.

Each grade began the same way and I urged Bubba to open up and sit with other kids. I could have cried (and probably did) when he came home visibly upset one day.

"Well I did try!" he yelled.

"What happened?" I asked.

"I put my tray and my stuff at a table with these other kids and went to get my milk. When I came back they had moved all my stuff to another table so I could sit by myself!"

Was he making this up? No. Was I misdirected in my approach? I felt sorry that I had pushed him, but I don't think there was misinterpretation on his part or my part about what transpired.

It wasn't too long after that when I stood behind two of his teammates at an indoor soccer game waiting for their team to show up.

Boy 1: "Where is everyone? Have you seen anybody from our team?"

Boy 2: "No. Well, Bubba is here." Giggle, giggle, eyes rolling. I was standing right behind them and didn't misinterpret anything.

As we visited our friends' homes on New Year's Eve one year I again, witnessed the ostracizing firsthand. We were at the home of the parents of one of the boys from Bubba's early days. Their boy "Charlie" had another friend over, and when we arrived they departed to go hang out in another part of the house without Bubba. Fortunately, Charlie's father, a good friend of mine, was able to subtly integrate the boys, and they played video games together later that evening.

It's really been a few close friends, family and the church that helped hold our social life together. It has taken a lot of encouragement to keep Bubba socially engaged. Not every kid can be popular of course, but it is hard to watch when your child is slowly separated from the pack and not necessarily in a way that would be considered positive. It was interesting that in a later grade, Bubba was mentoring special needs kids in a buddy program. I watched him treat the kids very nicely and converse with them one-on-one like a real special teenager would do.

Band and the Clarinet

> *Research has also suggested that a key to generalization and maintenance of any skill, whether it is taught as a component/tool skill or as part of a larger composite, is providing fluency-building practice that enables the student to perform the skill with accuracy and speed.*[15]

In fifth grade, the students were required to select choir, orchestra or band for a musical option as they prepared to move into middle school. Depending on the selection, this would be cheap, or this would be expensive. I didn't fully understand the consequences when Bubba selected band. Had I known, I might have pushed harder for choir.

Upon selecting band, there was a big event in the fall of sixth grade where hundreds of young, middle schoolers came to the school one evening to try out different instruments. The instrument vendors were on hand to provide information, instruments, and financing information. I steered Bubba towards the drums thinking that drums would be a natural for him. This was the little angel who pulled every pot and pan out of

---

[15] William L. Heward, "Ten Faulty Notions About Teaching and Learning That Hinder the Effectiveness of Special Education," *The Journal of Special Education*, 36 (4), 2003.

the cupboard and banged on them for hours every day when he was younger.

No. No drums. He went straight for the oboe.

Oddly enough he played the oboe on the first try. The teacher that was present (who I later discovered was a music store salesperson disguised as a teacher) oooed and ahhed over my precious child's natural talent. However, students didn't get to start on an oboe; they had to first "master the clarinet." I should have thanked her for steering us to the cheaper instrument.

Fortunately, there was a payment plan and insurance for the instrument. Unfortunately, I later discovered, when Bubba's band career was over, they don't buy the instruments back. That's apparently what E-bay is for. Net loss – approximately $700. Not counting reeds. Busted parts. Cleaning and adjustments.

Anyway, one day in sixth grade, Bubba came home without the clarinet. I asked him what had happened to it and he said the case opened as he was leaving his seat to exit the bus and parts rolled everywhere, under the seats. The bus driver, being on a tight schedule, made him get off the bus even though various parts were missing. We had to get into the car, drive to the bus depot and retrieve all the parts. Thank goodness they were all there. This was only the beginning of the clarinet trauma.

I remembered one night I asked Bubba to show me what he was learning. He was unable to play the clarinet. Shortly thereafter, I received a call from the band director. "Mama Bear," he said. "Bubba is not doing too well in band. I don't think it is financially prudent for him to continue."

I can tell you, band is not financially prudent. Period.

"How are you teaching him to play?" I innocently inquired. "He doesn't seem to be getting it."

"Well, he doesn't seem to be learning with the group, so I have placed him in another room where he can learn."

"Who's in there with him?" I asked. A funny, itchy, nervous feeling started to creep in; my heart sank; and anger ignited because I had a feeling I already knew the answer.

"He's by himself," the director reported.

"And what is he doing in the room by himself?" I asked, already knowing that the chances were pretty good he was sleeping or just sitting there.

"He's just sitting there," the instructor stated, very matter-of-factly. Amazing.

Now wouldn't you think that if a kid is not learning in the group, he probably isn't going to learn sitting in a room by himself? And, if the child is "learning disabled," wouldn't you think there is just no possibility he would learn sitting in a room by himself? Don't kids have to be able to read music; and is that something kids learn on their own? Okay, is that something most kids learn to do on their own?

"Put him back in with the group," I told the instructor.

Every good boy deserves fudge. Every good boy deserves fudge. E-G-B-D-F on the music scale. Over and over, and with about fifteen minutes a day of practicing at home, in about three months, Bubba was "clarinetting" with the class. I had played the clarinet for three years (a hundred years ago). It just wasn't that hard to teach Bubba how to play and I didn't think I was going to get much help from the band director. Once Bubba had the basics, he was able to hang with the class, though he wasn't sitting in first chair.

I didn't become a good friend or a big fan of the band director. Bubba told me once that the director was 94 years old. When I met him in person at the parent-teacher conference, I noticed he was pretty old. I understood later why he looked at me funny when I asked him if he was really 94 years old and congratulated him on his age.

It wasn't until spring that the real clarinet trauma unfolded and it couldn't have come at a worse time. Yes, my little angel had received a three day in-school suspension the week before the spring sixth-grade band concert. He was "bullying" another child to get food. Actually, he was asking the other child for his food at lunch time.

Ex and I had been summoned to the middle school to meet with the vice principal. "Bubba is making the other child miserable and he is home crying every night," the vice principal told us. We were seated in his office getting a good scolding.

"The other child's mother told me everything was fine." I replied nonchalantly.

"Why are you talking to the other child's mother?" I seemed to have broken some rule where parents shouldn't talk to each other. Veins were bulging in the man's forehead. Why was he getting so mad?

I ignored his spasm. "Bubba's only doing what I told him to do. I told him to ask and not just take other people's food. What am I supposed to punish him for?" My son was literally following my rule. (He was very literal, after all.) I had neglected to tell Bubba to only ask once and if the other person says no, give up.

Ex chimed in. "I've known this kid for twelve years, and one thing he is not, is a bully." Ex sunk lower in his chair and gave off the evil-eye.

"What about band?" I panicked. "Can he still practice with the group? The concert is next Tuesday." Funny, itchy, nervous feeling.

"Yes. He can practice with the band. We could have made this an out-of-school suspension, you know." The vice principal was letting us know who was boss. Ex and I removed ourselves from the room, saving our curse words until we were far away from the building and in the parking lot.

I tried reminding the vice principal about band practice that week, leaving e-mails and phone messages. I had asked Bubba about his suspension and whether he was practicing with the band and he said no, the suspension teacher wouldn't let him. I attempted contacting the vice principal again and couldn't get a call back.

Bubba did not get to practice for the spring band concert with the rest of the band.

So that is how the clarinet trauma unfolded in its entirety at the sixth grade spring concert. Proud parents in the stands. Squeaking instruments. Kids filing into a hot, crowded gymnasium. Chairs being rearranged and the tapping by the band director for attention. A hush came over the crowd and the director took the microphone, thanked everyone for attending, and announced his musical selections.

Parents fanned themselves with folded programs as the first number began. I saw Bubba fumbling with the music. It fell from the music stand to the floor. He bent to pick up the scattering of music sheets and finally placed them back in order on his stand. He looked around the room and we shared a glance. I could tell he was lost.

By the second number, he adopted a slumped posture and sank lower in his chair. He played a couple of notes but then looked lost again. I sat helpless in the stands.

By the third number, he had sank as low in his chair as possible without sliding completely off. And by the fourth number, tears were streaming down his face.

We hurriedly exited the building at the break and Bubba, in the midst of tears proclaimed, "I hate band." Justified or unjustified, the rage in my heart was intense. How does a parent fix a situation like that? What do you say? What was learned?

The answer is simple. There are some things a parent can't fix.

There was no appropriate response and there was absolutely nothing learned. I did what any other parent would do, and forced him to participate in band for two more years, following the "get back on the horse" philosophy. I taught him how to "fake it till you make it" if he got lost during a performance. He was a bundle of nerves at the first concert in seventh grade, but he made it through.

Note: Bubba received one of a handful of awards at the beginning of seventh grade for exhibiting the characteristics of integrity, honesty, and caring. This award was given by the teaching faculty a mere sixth months after he served the three–day suspension for "bullying."

The end of eighth grade was the official end of the clarinet trauma and the not-so-financially prudent band experience. Bubba and I both sighed sighs of relief as we closed the book on band.

Every good boy deserves fudge. Every good boy deserves a future.

Middle School, Lockers and Occupational Therapy

> *Most primary schools teach children in inclusive classrooms except for physical education and special classes like music and art. But in middle school, most children move from teacher to teacher, making it necessary to find classrooms all over the school building in what may only be a short time allowed between bells.*[16]

Middle school was horrifying, at least for me. I can not express any better word for those years, unless we substitute "torturous," perhaps. Relying on expert advice and intuition, we purchased all the school supplies for sixth grade early and took the supplies to school early, before the official start of the school year. Bubba and I found his locker, a half-height, bottom-row, middle of the section, five-inch wide metal trauma zone. Holding various books and trying to manipulate the combination did not work for him, so he sat on the floor to maintain stability while attempting to open the locker. As his hand had a mild tremor, getting the combination dial to stop on the exact line that marked a number, proved to be a challenge. After several attempts and practice, it seemed he had mastered opening the locker. We came back another day to make sure.

---

[16] Marcia Brown Rubinstien, *Raising NLD Superstars* (London: Jessica Kingsley Publishers, 2005).

All that good planning fell apart the first day of school, however, as the students had about five minutes to get to the locker, open the locker, exchange materials and get to the next class. With about thirty students in one small section, vying for their lockers simultaneously, and with some students opening the upper row of locker doors while others bent to retrieve materials from the lower row, it was mass chaos. That first day I watched Bubba attempt to get close to his locker and saw the challenge. He wasn't the type of kid to bust his way through the crowd with an attitude of "get outta my way." He stood back to wait until the other students cleared the area. Around the time the bell rang, he was working on the combination, finally got the locker open and arrived late to class. I hoped that things would get better as the year progressed, left for work and tried not to worry.

After getting several tardy reports and detentions for being late to class, apparently one of the teachers decided to reassign Bubba to an upper level locker on the end of a row. This may also have been after he received a head bruise from getting hit by an open upper row locker door. After several more tardy reports and detentions for being late to class and several visits by the school janitor to determine the problem with the locker, apparently one of the teachers then decided to have the lock cut off of the locker.

Bubba began coming home with new hats, shirts and other items. I asked him where he was getting the goods and he told me they were in his locker. It seems the other kids were placing items into the locker as it was not locked. I fretted about the seven-hundred-plus dollar clarinet that was sitting in there during the day, but we made it through the year without it getting heisted.

Sixth grade is when the schedule gets crazy. Instead of having a primary teacher, the students move from class to class and teacher to teacher, depending on the subject. I think that is confusing enough. But the schedule wasn't confusing enough for the middle school staff at Bubba's school.

Each day started at 7:30 a.m., except for Wednesday, when school started at 8:40 a.m. There was a theory, I guess, that having the extra hour one day a week allowed the teachers to communicate about their students. Every Wednesday, I was an hour late to work. Every Wednesday I presume many people were an hour late to work.

That wasn't crazy enough though. Each regular day consisted of eight or nine periods of forty minutes each, plus lunch. But Wednesday and Thursday were declared block days, where the nine periods were stretched to roughly two hours each and spread across the two days. For most of the classes, anyway. So Monday, Tuesday and Friday were on one schedule, and Wednesday and Thursday were on their own schedule. And Wednesday started an hour later than usual.

But that wasn't enough craziness either. In addition to this "regular" schedule, there were "A" and "B" days. I still don't get it. On an "A" day, a student might have band on the first period, but on a "B" day the student might have physical education. And the schedule didn't go "A","B","A","B". There was a monthly calendar sent home that showed the random assignment of "A" and "B" to the regular Monday/Tuesday/Friday schedule and the Wednesday/Thursday block (late start on Wednesday) schedule. That was the "normal" middle school schedule, not counting holiday weeks or exam weeks or snow days, which could change everything.

Of course, Bubba might not have his gym clothes on the correct day or might be missing his instrument on a band day. I received notes about this and emails from the teachers wondering why he didn't always come prepared for class. Pulling my hair out over the schedule (while Bubba would look at me and say "Tomorrow is a block day, 'A' and I have don't have math on Wednesdays Mom"), I decided to just send gym clothes, all his books and his clarinet every day. Bubba was carrying about fifty pounds in his book bag.

Sixth grade was the year of detentions. One time Bubba got a detention for being late for a detention, when he was on a field trip with his class that was late returning to school. I spoke to the vice principal but he shrugged his shoulders and just looked at me when I pointed this out.

"What do you want me to do?" he asked.

I couldn't really get too concerned about the detentions. What I did get concerned about was Bubba's attitude. It began to deteriorate. His handwriting was poor and his math skills were lacking.

I wrote sixth grade off as a transition year. I hoped seventh grade would be better, but it wasn't.

One day in the seventh grade, the occupational therapist called me to discuss some behavior outbursts that Bubba was expressing in one of his classes. Bubba didn't like how the student next to him laid his book bag in Bubba's work space. Bubba was pushing it out of his space with his foot and not paying attention during class. This didn't sound like occupational therapy to me and what did they want me to do – come to school and yell at him?

I asked the occupational therapist how the handwriting instruction was going. She replied, "Am I supposed to be working on that?" It was written in his IEP program that he would see the occupational therapist twice a week to work on handwriting as it was barely legible. Yes, she was supposed to be working on that. The goal specifically addressed the legibility of Bubba's handwriting, including spacing, size and proportion.

"What are you doing with him exactly?" I asked.

"I help him on the computer," she replied.

"Are you teaching him to type?"

"No."

"What exactly are you doing then?"

"I watch him type or work on the computer," she finally confessed.

I asked to see her logs for sixth and seventh grade. These are actual excerpts from her occupational therapy log from sixth grade and for the first eight months of seventh grade:

- *Met with Bubba and his teacher.*
- *Bubba working by himself.*
- *Bubba using the computer to complete work.*
- *Bubba working on the computer. He became agitated that the headphones were not working properly.*
- *Locker difficulties.*
- *Handwritten work sloppy and large.*
- *Cleaned out locker.*
- *Not using locker.*

- *Class worked on essays today.*
- *Holiday.*
- *Back from vacation. Attempting to get into routine.*
- *Set-up laptops.*
- *No school holiday.*
- *Teacher created page for class to use.*
- *Teacher wanting to have students read the book.*
- *Caseload not seen due to exams and altered schedule.*
- *Bubba reports no problems.*
- *This teacher attended a conference and was not in attendance this week.*
- *Lunch room observation.*
- *No OT.*
- *Achievement testing.*
- *No OT. Therapist assisting with testing at high school.*
- *Concern: one student inviting other class members to his home, always in earshot of Bubba and he has never been invited.*
- *Class attended local restaurant.*

There were about fifty entries on the occupational therapist's log for the entire sixth and seventh grade, none of which appeared to involve any direct instruction in his handwriting or fine motor skills, and very few that even referenced Bubba directly. I called District Administrator 2 who informed me that Bubba would never learn to write cursive, and his handwriting was not improving and, they weren't going to spend any more time on it.

Note: There was no law that would force them to teach him cursive as in many states cursive learning is optional. The teaching of cursive is not in the Common Core State Standards, a list of grade-by-grade objectives for English and mathematics adopted by the public school systems in many states.[17] The handwriting goals were listed in the IEP and it was a violation of the law for District Administrator 2 to declare unilaterally that they were abandoning the goal.[18] I knew at that time that the

---

[17] National Governors Association Center for Best Practices, Council of Chief State School Officers, "Common Core State Standards," Washington D.C., 2010.

[18] See 34 CFR 300.324(a)(4). "In making changes to a child's IEP after the annual IEP Team meeting for a school year, the parent of a child with a

unilateral decision didn't sound legal, but I didn't *know* that or understand what to do about it.

Since they weren't going to teach him how to write, I requested that they teach Bubba how to type. There was a definite shift in the occupational therapist's log entries after this point as she began teaching him how to type.

Log entries after I expressed my concern read:

- *Discussed Bubba using the typing program – installed on computer.*
- *Typing program – Bubba typed with 95% accuracy.*
- *Typing program – 96% accuracy.*
- *Class working on report writing.*
- *Typing program – 95% accuracy.*
- *Typing program – good effort for first five minutes.*
- *Class field trip.*

There was some attempt to teach him how to type, but by this time, the seventh grade school year was almost ending. Instead of modifying his programming and adding typing, we skipped that process and the team asked me to take the typing program and something called a Neo home for the summer so I could teach him at home.

It was around this time that I felt there were too many lost opportunities for Bubba. He was losing confidence in himself; I was losing confidence in the school; and there was only one year of middle school left, four years of high school, and then what?

---

disability and the public agency may agree not to convene an IEP Team meeting for the purposes of making those changes, and instead may develop a written document to amend or modify the child's current IEP."

The Turning Point

> *If a boy is having trouble making friends, it helps most if he can be in a school and in a class where the program is flexible. It helps to put him in a seat next to a very popular child, or to let him be partners with him in activities going on errands around the school, etc.*[19]

I had heard it said that when the amount of pain reaches a certain point, motivation sets in. Bubba was in pain and I was in pain, unclear on what path to take or even what to do.

I began reading, researching through books and the internet about the behaviors Bubba had exhibited, and the strengths and weaknesses of his educational profile; I began rereading all the school evaluations and supplementary information from the special education reports that had been performed.

I called the State Special Education Advocacy Group and talked to a counselor. She made the simple statement that "No one knows your son better than you do." I was starting to really believe it. I was in tears while I talked to her, because I had been feeling so confused and

---

[19] Benjamin Spock M.D. and Michael B. Rothenberg, *Dr. Spock's Baby and Child Care. Sixth Edition* (New York: Simon & Schuster, 1992).

frustrated and finally I felt like I had found someone who understood what I was talking about. She also advised me to thoroughly read and understand the parent's rights documents and mentioned the idea of requesting mediation or filing a complaint.

The school district had applied the label of cognitive disability to Bubba in his fourth grade evaluation review. This was because I questioned the label of a non-specific, specific learning disability. So one day, as I was reading the special education handbook definitions and following the advice of the advocate, I found that the term cognitive disability was an updated, replacement label for mentally retarded.

I knew without a doubt by this time that the school district had incorrectly identified Bubba's disability category and was unsure what to do about it. I knew I couldn't let the school district perform his next evaluation. They would not even consider categorizing him with the label that I was beginning to know was correct and I would not even consider letting him remain categorized with the cognitive disability label that I now understood to be the equivalent of mentally retarded. It wasn't that I couldn't accept their classification, if it was correct, but I knew that a child with a solidly normal verbal IQ didn't qualify as cognitively disabled.

I contacted District Coordinator 2 at the end of the sixth grade year to let her know that I was going to have Bubba independently evaluated. I desperately wanted Bubba's evaluation performed by a specialist who was not employed by the school district, because it seemed like the independent evaluator we had used in the first grade was better qualified and did a more thorough job than the school district's psychologist. In addition, the independent psychologist miraculously came up with scores that were very different from the school district scores.

I contacted the Children's Hospital again for a recommendation for a neuropsychological evaluation for Bubba. They provided me with a list of two specialists, and after some background research, I selected NeuroPsych. He was a PhD-level neuropsychologist who was well respected throughout the state. He sent information on what types of testing he would perform, explained over the phone that it would take several days and involve supplementary information from Bubba's teachers, and quoted his price. It was expensive.

So I contracted independently with NeuroPsych to get Bubba evaluated before the school made their attempt to evaluate him.

It took a month or two on the waiting list to get Bubba in to see NeuroPsych, but late in the summer, before seventh grade began, we were able to get on his schedule. We had an initial consult on the first day and then the testing began. This continued over the course of several days, and took up most of a working day for each session. It was somewhat tiring for Bubba, I could see, but he did seem to enjoy the sessions because NeuroPsych had a way of making them fun.

School started back up in the meantime and it was back to middle school for Bubba. I was able to collect information from Bubba's teachers that NeuroPsych requested and forward that onward to him. These were a series of behavioral assessments that, combined with the parental assessments, helped the evaluator to gain a broader perspective of Bubba in different environments.

Once the testing was completed and all the supplementary information was collected, I met with NeuroPsych to go over the results. After a brief exchange of "How are you doing," NeuroPsych laid a bomb on me! He asked me if I wanted to be a neuropsychologist; and how did I know Bubba had this rare type of disability? The disability was only present in around one in a thousand students.

He went over the test results, explaining in complicated terms, much of what I had already come to understand. NeuroPsych called the current school programming and their categorization of Bubba as cognitively disabled a "tragedy" and asked me to set up an evaluation review session where he could come to the school immediately to speak with Bubba's seventh grade teachers.

About two weeks later, NeuroPsych came to the school to meet with Bubba's team and the special education staff. District Coordinator 2 was present, as well as Bubba's science teacher, the special education teacher and the occupational therapist. He explained how Bubba's verbal capabilities, spelling and basic reading were his strengths, and the difficulties Bubba had interpreting pictures and graphs. NeuroPsych talked about Bubba's literalness, social difficulties and how easy it was to have misunderstandings with Bubba.

One test NeuroPsych covered was the *Rey-Osterrieth Complex Figure Test*.[20] This test was designed to evaluate a child's level of visual-spatial perception, construction and the ability to recall a visual image. With this test, the child examines a picture, is asked to copy the picture, and then recall the picture from memory. Later they are asked to perform what is called a delayed recall, when he or she is tasked with drawing the picture from memory after some time has passed. (I can't remember the exact delay, it may be about 30 minutes.)[21]

A copy of the picture is shown next that is used for the testing.

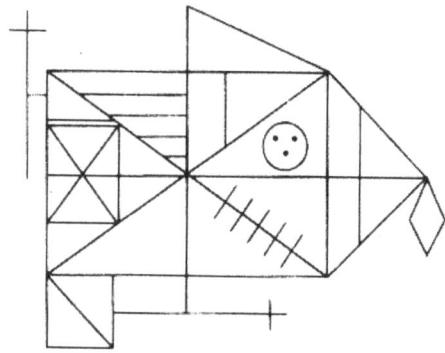

Rey-Osterrieth Complex Figure Test Picture

When NeuroPsych presented Bubba's version of the drawing from recall, there was a lot of interest from the science teacher. Bubba's version did not look much like the test picture. He had separated the figure into respective parts (boxes, lines, crosses) and had organized them into groups of like parts.

The science teacher immediately grasped the information being relayed and the difficulties Bubba would have with pictures and graphs. She appeared excited to understand some of the problems Bubba was having

---

[20] PA Osterrieth, "Le Test de Copie d'une Figure Complexe," *Archives of Psychology*, 30:206–356, 1944.

[21] M. Lipowska, E. Czaplewska, and A. Wysocka, "Visual-Spatial Deficits of Dyslexic Children," *Medical Science Monitor* (17) 4, April, 2011.

in her class. "I've been using pictures to try to explain concepts to him. No wonder he looks more confused!" In contrast to the science teacher, the special education teacher didn't appear to grasp any concepts, and seemed more intent on pushing back her cuticles and examining her nail polish.

NeuroPsych warned everyone about potential increased depression and anxiety with Bubba, and how it was common for uncommon kids like Bubba. He recommended a buddy or check-in person for Bubba when he came to speak to Bubba's team at school. They all shook their heads "yes" and spent some time discussing options for implementing a buddy for Bubba.

The occupational therapist seemed interested in the visual-spatial difficulties and NeuroPsych presented ideas and tools that would be useful for Bubba. There was a sense of excitement in the room, a sense that so many of Bubba's difficulties were explainable, and that there were specific methods available to improve Bubba's programming.

District Coordinator 2 was fairly silent throughout the session. She did acknowledge NeuroPsych's request to have his evaluation of Bubba serve as a substitute for the school's evaluation. The school district's evaluation is required by law to be performed every three years.[22] The team all signed the evaluation and the corresponding change of Bubba's special education categorization. I left the school that day feeling optimistic and empowered that I was able to help the school district personnel provide better help for my son, get Bubba's label changed, and that there would be changes to his programming so his comfort level at school would improve.

Unfortunately, even after the visit, the evaluation and the explanations by this well-respected neuropsychologist, there was no change in Bubba's programming.

I asked his special education teacher if Bubba could get challenge words on his weekly spelling tests. The four-letter spelling words were boring

---

[22] See 34 CFR 300.303(b)(2) - Reevaluations. "Must occur at least once every 3 years, unless the parent and the public agency agree that a reevaluation is unnecessary."

him and he had never gotten less than 100% on the quizzes. NeuroPsych had explained pretty clearly that Bubba was around four levels above grade in spelling.

"No," she replied. "He needs to firm up his spelling skills." So much for that suggestion. But I am persistent. After a month or two, I approached her again and got the same response. Finally, after six months of Bubba consistently receiving 100% on the four-letter spelling word quizzes, she added two challenge words, especially for him. They weren't challenging enough and he continued to complain regularly about how boring school was.

The teacher finally made Bubba's spelling lists all challenge words (this must have caused some confusion and extra work), but he still flew through the quizzes and was bored. I asked if he could get extra help on his math weaknesses and skip the spelling and finally, towards the end of seventh grade he was exempt from spelling quizzes. While the other students were taking their spelling tests, Bubba spent the quiz time independently working on math, which I was pretty certain was not too effective either. He needed to be taught math and I was coming to the conclusion he wasn't going to get taught math at school.

Over the course of the next few months, I repeatedly asked for a buddy for Bubba and was finally told he could go see the counselor whenever he wanted. There was no movement on that front – it had all been just talk. I scratched my head and began asking more questions and formulating a more aggressive approach to change.

"Black and White"

Part 2 – Interventions and Meetings

The turning point was really when I began to lose confidence in the ability of the special education system to provide a proper education for Bubba. For example, the school district personnel had identified him incorrectly, made declarations of "never" that were evidently incorrect, and had ignored the advice from a well-respected professional (NeuroPsych). Now I began to start documenting my requests in writing. I began teaching cursive to Bubba immediately, not because it was the most important skill that he needed, but because I needed to understand why, after several years, the occupational therapists had been unable to make progress. Teaching Bubba cursive provided a glimmer of knowledge that led to a series of activities that helped me understand how Bubba learned.

I could see that he had great difficulty taking what he saw with his eyes and translating those images into physical representations on paper using a pencil held in his hand. I watched this difficulty as it happened. Several related deficiencies in his interpretation of the concept of magnitude became apparent. My understanding grew and the activities we did together at home were designed to incorporate his strong verbal capabilities and remediate, or work around his difficulties.

Conversely, the school district continued to provide interventions that were not in the IEP using the same methods they had always used.

These types of interventions were designed for students with strong visual-spatial capabilities, reading and spelling difficulties, and the types of special education students they were familiar with instructing. And meanwhile they forgot to provide interventions that *were* in the IEP.

Part 2 describes the meetings and interventions we participated in during middle school and high school. Part 3 describes the activities and strategies I pursued to better understand and exercise my parental rights while Bubba was in middle school and high school.

The Letter Writing Begins

My frustration by the end of seventh grade and the downward spiral of Bubba's academics and demeanor prompted me to initiate several actions. Instead of relying on telephone conversations, I began to write letters that were fact-based with reminders of the recommendations that were included in NeuroPsych's evaluation. The requests were primarily focused on addressing Bubba's weak areas because I was becoming convinced that the school district had no intentions of addressing them. I wanted the recommendations addressed.

So the first letter writing effort is shown below. The school district felt that because NeuroPsych had visited in the fall, we didn't need to have another IEP meeting, even though I requested one. I wanted to discuss extended year services (services over the summer), issues with services identified in the IEP that were not being provided, and Bubba's lack of progress during the year. The district did not provide any reason for their refusal (a reason for refusal would be a Prior Written Notice) and tried to ignore my request. This is in conflict with *IDEA*.[23]

---

[23] See CFR Section 300.324(b)(1). It states that the Public Agency "Reviews the child's IEP periodically, but not less than annually, to determine whether the annual goals for the child are being achieved;" and "Revises the IEP, as appropriate, to address (A) Any lack of expected progress toward the annual goals described in Sec. 300.320(a)(2), and in the general education curriculum,

I had seen another year wasted, where the school district ignored NeuroPsych's evaluation, even though they had accepted it as their own. They had accepted his change in disability designation, but had neglected to update his IEP.

> *Hi.*
>
> *I would like to make sure that we have Bubba's IEP this spring, prior to the completion of seventh grade. I am planning on using a tutor over the summer and would like to target that appropriately and get his schedule in place for 8th grade as well. His IEP should reflect the change in designation of disability and it is important that the IEP be reworked to reflect the specifics of his disability and the recommended accommodations for his designation.*
>
> *There are several issues that need resolved. I believe Bubba is supposed to be receiving occupational therapy for 30 minutes each week and I am not sure that is happening. I have not received any report pertaining to this. His handwriting needs work and keyboard instruction should be part of his IEP as well going forward.*
>
> *We discussed a buddy system for Bubba at the meeting in the fall and I don't believe there has been any progress in that area either. NeuroPsych indicated the importance of identifying a compassionate buddy that Bubba can check in with each day. This will be extremely important for next year as well.*
>
> *The effectiveness of the resource room is questionable. This year he has been given word lists for spelling that seriously under-challenge one of his personal strengths. Approximately two hours per week of time at home is spent copying these*

---

if appropriate;
(B) The results of any reevaluation conducted under Sec. 300.303;
(C) Information about the child provided to, or by, the parents, as described under Sec. 300.305(a)(2);
(D) The child's anticipated needs; or
(E) Other matters." The parents and district can agree not to meet but the district must respond to the parent's request for an IEP meeting.

words, finding their meanings in the dictionary and creating crossword puzzles (or other activities) related to these words, yet he has been successfully spelling these words since the second grade. The time spent on homework should be spent in areas of his greatest weakness (math) so he can get one-on-one time.

The usefulness of the resource room for math is questionable as well. It is not effective for him to do 20 or 30 problems all wrong without correction; an incorrect process should be corrected immediately for him to gain consistency in the correct process.

In terms of scheduling for next year I would like Bubba to be removed from resource room instruction. This has not been an effective strategy and it is time to rethink modifications. I would also like to quantify the gap between what Bubba understands in math and what is expected from an 8th grade math student so that concepts can be prioritized and addressed through school instruction, home instruction and tutoring.

Suggestions for IEP – these are from NeuroPsych's report:

- *Direct instruction and remediation of his organization, planning and self-monitoring. This should include use of an organizer or journal to write down assignments, due dates and materials needed. Daily oversight should be provided until Bubba does this for himself. Bubba should have at least one supported study hall where he can work with an adult to assist him with assignment management. Journal entry each day with identification of materials needed, assignments due with clear due dates (due Monday, September x, 20xx).*

- *Homework should be limited and focused primarily on math. Math teacher should work closely with parents who provide one-on-one home instruction to support class work.*

- *Bubba should be placed near the front of the classroom with a clear view of the teacher and the board and free from distractions.*

- *Whenever possible Bubba should be given assignments in advance (either the week before or by Monday for assignments due during the week). Communication via email between school and home including homework assignments with stated due date (due Monday, September x, 20xx).*

- *Buddy system implemented within the first 2 weeks of school for every class in which Bubba is included. The proposed buddy should have the character quality of compassion and assist with any locker issues, room location or other expected confusion. NeuroPsych also suggests that social problems are a core area of deficit and recommends that he have a check-in person to assist with social functioning and adaptation to school stress.*

- *Keyboarding instruction. Goal should be improving keyboarding skills and measurable in words per minute.*

- *Social skill training and behavior monitoring. Weekly or bi-weekly meeting with guidance counselor to discuss social issues, behavior issues and enact role playing for situations encountered in the school setting.*

- *Preview of 8th grade materials. We can use these materials over the summer to give him a head start.*

- *Tardy accommodation.*

- *Two sets of books where necessary. A copy of books needed at school will be provided for home use as well.*

- *When a written examination is administered, teacher or aide checks over exam before the test is turned in for completeness to make sure Bubba has read the questions correctly in giving his answer. Tests modified/shortened such that most important concepts are identified for priority. NeuroPsych also suggested that Bubba be graded on the amount of work he is able to complete in a given time period.*

- *Occupational therapy 30 minutes per week. Continued work on handwriting for neatness. Continued work on cursive.*

- *Minimize copying from the board or books. Problems should be photocopied and handouts/notes provided by teacher.*

The net result of this letter was that we finally had the IEP meeting, and the special education teacher admitted that she was only able to spend about fifteen minutes a week one-on-one with Bubba. The occupational therapist and school principal (who later became Assistant District Superintendent) declared that he would never be able to write cursive and they were not going to try to teach it to him anymore.

There was no provision for working with Bubba over the summer to get him caught up with math, but it was the beginning of a successful removal of Bubba from the resource room, the one effort that helped bring his attitude around. He pleaded with me that he would "rather get Cs and Ds in the regular classroom than As or Bs in the resource room."

Even though the requests included in the letter were the priorities established in NeuroPsych's evaluation report - the report that the district adopted as their evaluation, the priorities were mostly ignored by the school district personnel. Indeed there was a reason why virtually all the requests could not be implemented. I was assured that the teaching staff was following the existing IEP and that Bubba was doing just fine.

It's not clear to me why the district's members of the IEP team ignored most of the requests, I suppose because I let them. I knew that what I was asking for was simply what the expert had recommended, but I still felt powerless and that maybe I was just asking for too much. I was also becoming concerned that even if I fought for all these accommodations, the district was not likely to follow up and implement them anyway.

To not go away empty handed, I continued the meeting into the third hour. I had lost the cursive battle, was handed over the responsibility of teaching him keyboarding, had been notified that foreign language was something that Bubba could never learn, and had been turned down repeatedly by a team of professionals who were unified in their mission. But, by the third hour, they had started to weaken. It was at this point that I recognized that the longer I sat in a meeting, the more likely it was that I would get something I wanted. But to get everything from NeuroPsych's recommendations might have taken weeks.

After a lengthy argument, I was finally able to get Bubba out of the resource room for reading, an effort that I continued in subsequent dealings with the school administration until he was out for all classes. The resource room may be effective for some kids, but for Bubba it was not working. His reading was average to above average before he entered the resource room. His grade level gains dropped to less than a grade per year once he was there. I would have stayed another hour or two, or even more, if needed just to accomplish that single feat.

Statistical Note on Children Returning to Regular Education

Return to regular education – Kids moving out of special education and returning to regular education status went from around 4% in 1998 to less than 3% in 2008 (for the ages 14-21).

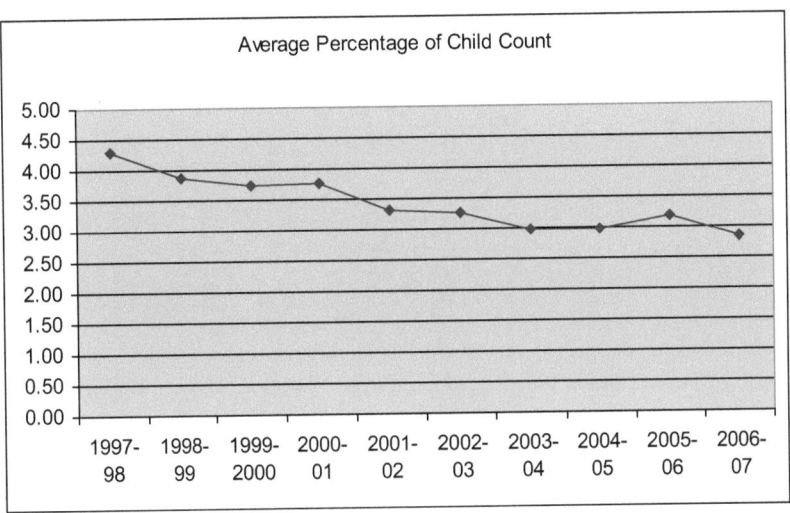

Average Percentage of Special Education Students Returned to Regular Education[24]

Most children aren't returned to regular education; they stay in special education (around 97% of special education kids). It doesn't seem too likely then, that if a child is moved into special education that he or she will ever graduate back to general education, even though the intent of the special education may be to improve the child's skill such that they do not need special education. The odds are against it, and the odds are slowly getting worse.

---

[24] Office of Special Education Programs, U.S. Department of Education. "Children with Disabilities Exiting Special Education - 1998-99 to 2006-07."

Learning Cursive

Handwriting process instruction would be important for children even if written work would all be produced on a word processor![25]

As Bubba was finishing his seventh grade school year, and after seven years of special education and occupational therapy, school personnel had given up on teaching him how to write. We determined that improvement in keyboarding skills was necessary as it is important for a child to have some medium where he can write and express his thoughts, as other children are capable of doing. Comments from Bubba's teachers and the occupational therapist in the end-of-year IEP meeting were along the lines of "teaching a blind person to write," and the school staff did not have any hope of conquering the teaching of cursive hand-writing to Bubba. One teacher stated that being able to write cursive "is not really necessary anymore" and the promise of technology was forwarded as a practical substitute for hand-writing.

The situation reminded me of a manager that I was assigned to once. I really thought he was an idiot and I usually don't come to that type of

---

[25] Charles H. Trafford and Rand H. Nelson, "We Write To Read: Research Based Instruction for Handwriting Process, Book Two: Cursive Readiness," *Peterson Directed Handwriting*, 1996.

conclusion quickly. Another co-worker had worked for him, so I consulted with the co-worker on how he had managed the idiot manager. He said, "Shake your head 'yes' and then do the right thing." Now this fellow was a lot younger than I was so I partially followed his advice. I went ahead and did the right thing but called the idiot manager out as an idiot to the senior level management. That was more my style.

About the same time as the IEP meeting, I witnessed Bubba perform beautifully at his Bar-Mitzvah. He gave a six-page speech that engaged and entertained an audience of about 50 people, and stunned his grandfather, grandmother, Rabbi, father and mother as well as other people who were aware of his challenges. His delivery was that of a trained speaker, polished and eloquent. As I watched and assisted in his writing of thank-you notes, the stark difference between the speaking child and the writing child could not have been more pronounced.

I could not give up on the hope that Bubba would be able to sign his name. I could not believe that he would not have a need to at least be able to read cursive someday and I could not live with myself if I didn't take a shot at teaching him how to write. The idea of technology providing complete substitution for writing ability did not ring true.

So flash forward to six months after the IEP meeting. Some parents might fret when they are handed a yellow detention sheet from their child because it means there was some inappropriate incident that day at school. Not me. When I looked at Bubba's signature at the bottom of the detention slip I smiled, because he wrote his own name beautifully in cursive. I told him so and he said "I know." He confidently wrote in cursive, and while it was not as eloquent as his Bar-Mitzvah speech, it was certainly legible and a better reflection of the person called Bubba.

The resources I used to teach cursive to Bubba follow.

- *The Peterson Guide for Left-Handed Writers*
- *Why Johnny Can't Read and What You Can Do About It*[26]
- Two Primary Tablets with 7/8" Guideline Ruling
- College-Rule Paper and pencils
- A hand-made chart of the cursive letters

---

[26] Rudolf Flesch, *Why Johnny Can't Read: And What You Can Do About It* (Harper & Row Publishers, Inc., 1955).

The *Peterson Guide* was a document I had sent away for years ago. It had practical tips on the push-pull movement of the pencil, paper placement and basic ergonomic principles that assist with hand-writing. The push-pull method was the starting point for us, beginning with the letters "l" and "e".

The book *Why Johnny Can't Read and What You Can Do About It* was in our home since first grade when I was informed my son would never read. This book has about 70 pages in the back that list phonic combinations and provide lots of sample words for each combination.

The primary tablets were what I used for all the initial work. I found that writing in the larger size was easier for Bubba than on college-rule paper. This necessitated a strategy for moving from the large size to the small size handwriting.

The hand-made chart of cursive letters was NOT used as a tool for him to look at and copy from. What we did use it for was a rating tool. Bubba would rate how he felt he was doing on each letter as we started practicing the letter and then later as we reviewed the letters. He took responsibility for assessing his progress and seemed happy to do the assessment. He used terms like "NW" for "needs work," or "GBNW" for "good but needs work," and "A" or "AAA" if he felt he had mastered the letter.

Overcoming the Writing Phobia - My son had developed a phobia about writing after experiencing so much disappointment in his earlier education. Getting him to take on the challenge involved a discussion. I was very upfront with him about what I wanted to do and extracted a commitment from him to hang in there with me. The primary tool that I used to overcome this phobia was to keep the sessions very short, regular, but not every day. I would inform him that we were going to do a writing session, and that it would not take over ten minutes if he cooperated. I also informed him that it could take 20 to 30 minutes if he did not cooperate. We would look at the clock and figure out the estimated stop time. Most importantly, I kept my promise about the time spent per session. As he made progress and saw that I kept my promise, there was very little arguing about engaging in a writing session.

Using a Verbal Approach – The comments about "teaching a blind person to write" did not sit well with me, but there was a nugget of gold in the expression. Looking at letters that someone else had written, or samples on paper, or even tracing letters had not worked for Bubba. How would you teach a blind person to write? Copying and tracing would not work, so I employed a verbal approach. What that entailed was a verbal description of each letter, verbal directions on where the pencil needed to go – how high or how low, and where the cross-over point was supposed to be. Of course he is not blind and I used markings on the top, middle, bottom and below-the-line points to help guide the discussion about how a letter was supposed to be made.

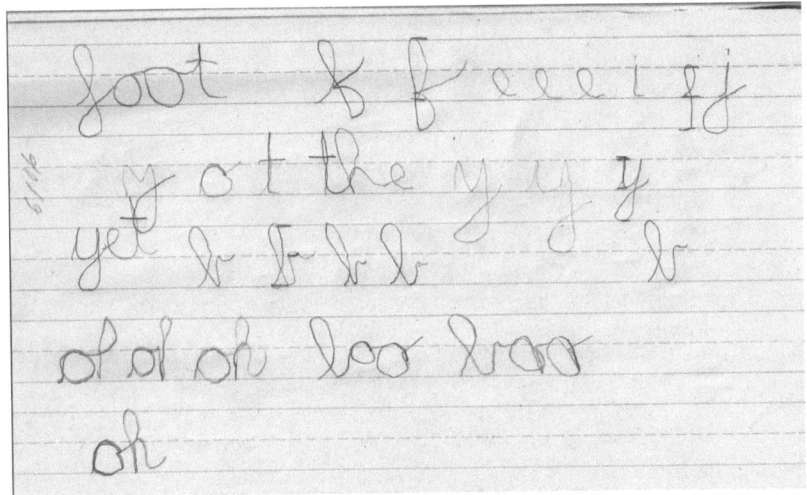

Early Attempts at Writing – Usage of Markings for Letter Drawing

In the previous figure, some of Bubba's earliest hand-writing attempts are shown. This was after using the *Peterson Guide* and the introduction of a few letters. Note the markings at the top, bottom and below-the-line on the letter "f" and "y". Also note the progression of the letter "y" from being way below the line, to being drawn correctly. After getting the "y" drawn correctly, he was able to successfully write the word "yet." This page represents about two ten-minute sessions. Letters like "o" and "b" were more challenging and it was during this process that it became apparent that transitioning from one letter to the next (or connecting the letters) would need an approach.

There were a series of terms I used to help describe letters, including:

- For letters like "l", "e", "b", and "k" a "loop" is involved. It might be a tall loop or a short loop. Using the terms "push" and "pull" were helpful, also for describing an upstroke and downstroke.

- Bubba's early attempts at the "t" and the "i" looked like an upside-down "v". I felt it was important to stop any drawing issues at the first opportunity – not to let him repeat an error more than once. I used an expression like "keep the legs together" and "go right back where you came from" to describe a tight "t" and "i".

- For letters like the "b", "v" and "w", I used the term "hand." The letter has "its hand out" and showed a cupped hand to help him visualize.

- For the "m", "n", and "h", I used the term "hump." To move from "h" to the "k", I used the term "squeeze in at the waist" and "tighten the belt" on the "h" to help him draw the "k".

Using these types of terms helped to lighten the atmosphere of the sessions, particularly in the early attempts, as I wanted to make them as short and as fun as possible.

The process broke down into five phases. I didn't really know what I was doing when I started, but the phases evolved as we started into the sessions. I knew the first phase was to learn to write each of the small letters; so that is where we started.

The five phases were:

- Phase 1 – Small Letters and Common Words
- Phase 2 – Letter Combinations
- Phase 3 – Shrink to College Rule Paper
- Phase 4 – Capitals
- Phase 5 – Writing in Free Space or Un-Ruled Paper

There were also a few sessions dedicated to the writing of his signature. I explained to him how a signature is something to be proud of and how it represents him to other people. We looked at my signature and his dad's signature (which is barely legible) and how different people sign their name. I just felt it was important for him to think of his signature as something special. I realized after making a big deal about it, that if the writing process didn't work, and he wasn't able to write his signature, I would have saddled him with another writing failure. Fortunately that didn't happen and that may not have been the best approach. Who knows though, maybe it made us both more determined to accomplish the signature.

Phase 1 – Small Letters and Common Words

The first two letters we attempted were the "e" and the "l". An interesting insight into Bubba's disability emerged at the first lesson, just by attempting these two letters. I felt that they were great examples because they were fairly easy to describe and he could apply the concepts from the Peterson method. What I wasn't aware of until we attempted these two letters, was that he really didn't know what I meant when I said that the "e" was "half as big" as the "l". I had some awareness of a strangeness when Bubba described the heights of things, or used measurement terms, but it never really hit home until the "e" and the "l". There was an issue with magnitude that carried over into many aspects of his being, including his social skills.[27] It was at this point that I initiated the use of markings (as described earlier) to help display the difference between a letter of full-height and a letter of half-height.

The letters fall into families and so we tackled families of letters that have similar characteristics. The families I used and attempted in this order were:

---

[27] The magnitude issue was evident in Bubba's social skills as I would see him over-react to small slights by a friend he played with. This prompted me to use a term "Level 1," which is when someone says something that irritates you, or the person is "pushing your buttons." The term "Level 2" has a higher significance in that the person is being deliberately rude. This goes up to "Level 5" where someone is physically threatening to kill you.

- The loopy letters – "e", "l", "k", "h", "f", and "b"
- Letters with balls – "a", "d", "g", "o", "p", "c", and "q"
- Letters with hands – "v", "w", and "b" (again)
- Letters with dots – "i" and "j"
- Letters with humps – "m" and "n"
- Hard letters – "x", "y", and "z"

The "r", "s", "t" and "u" we fit in – I didn't really have a family for them. It took about two months to get through these letter families on the large-ruled paper using about three sessions of ten minutes each. The results are shown in the figure below.

Common words we addressed were "for", "the", "at", "it", "like" and "and" (there may have been a few others). I explained to Bubba that being able to write these words well would account for about half of the written language (I have no facts to support that) and would give him a boost for writing complete sentences.

I would present words using letters he had attempted as we went through the letter families. For example, after we finished the loopy family, I had him write the words "left" and "felt." This indicated the need for the second phase where the ability to transition from one letter to another looked problematic. The next figure shows early work on writing the small letters.

Writing the Small Letters

Note in the previous figure where the "p" is crossed out. I encouraged Bubba to cross out errors as opposed to erasing and writing over. When he erased work, there was more anger or frustration, and sometimes ripped paper that only contributed to his unease. When he crossed out errors he became less critical of himself and would shrug his shoulders and move on. The top portion of this figure was removed because it contained Bubba's signature.

Phase 2 – Letter Combinations

It became apparent that Bubba would need to practice common transitions because there was not an intuitive mechanism for him to put letters together. And for letter combinations like "br" or "be", specific discussion would be necessary as the hand of the "b" needed to be adjusted when it connected to the next letter.

I used the pages in the back of the *Why Johnny Can't Read and What You Can Do About It* book as the foundation for the letter combinations.

Within two weeks (or so) of finishing up Phase 1, Ex wanted to see what progress was made. He printed out a saying and asked Bubba to write it in cursive. This is shown in next figure.

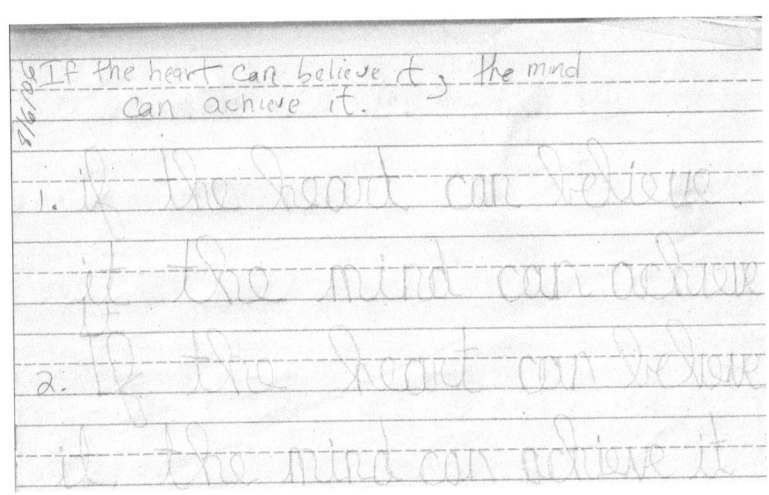

Writing Sample While in Phase 2

Note that capital letters don't come until a later phase, but the writing is pretty legible already and the transitions are good. We had tackled the "be" combination, but not the "ve" combination and there is a noticeable difference.

The following figure shows an example of how the combinations were presented. I would write the combination we were doing on the left-hand side of the paper. Bubba would make up a word that uses the combination (that was fun for him) and then write the word.

Using Phonic Combinations to Transition

If there were any serious problems, I would stop him and have him rework the word. We would tackle five or ten combinations in a session. I prepared the pages prior to a session.

Phase 3 – Shrink to College Rule Paper

This phase did not take long once I had an approach. In the previous phases, I had occasionally presented the college-rule paper and had Bubba try some words. The magnitude issue appeared again and what came out nicely on the large-ruled paper did not work on the college rule paper.

To help Bubba shrink his writing, I modified college-ruled paper by hand to look just like the larger-ruled paper. I drew a dotted line half-way between the lower line and the upper line. I also drew a dotted line for the below-the-line letters. Bubba was able to duplicate anything he had done on the large-ruled paper to the college-ruled paper when it was modified.

To transition from modified college-ruled paper, I simply began making the lines I added lighter and less noticeable. Within two weeks of finishing Phase 2, Bubba had completed Phase 3 (albeit a little shakily). He was able to write legibly on college-ruled paper.

The next figure is an example of one of the spelling tests from early in the eighth grade year. We started the process in the beginning of June and this test was from September. The quality of the cursive isn't perfect by any means, but it is very legible.

1. unquestionable
2. turbulence
3. Interstate
4. attack
5. indifferent
6. arsenal
7. independence
8. nonviolent
9. reforestation
10. nonreturnable return 15x
   nonreturnable

Sample Spelling Test after Completion of Phase 3

Phase 4 – Capitals

By the time we finished the third phase, it was time for Bubba to go back to school – in the eighth grade. For the most part, Bubba had been able to print his capital letters. I encouraged him to use a printed version of a capital letter for the first letter of his words because he was comfortable with that method.

Phase 5 - Writing in Free Space or Un-Ruled Paper

For writing in free space or un-ruled paper, I encouraged Bubba to draw a line first and then write what he needed to write. This was probably the biggest challenge, but is not used with much frequency. Cursive was not Bubba's favorite, but I did make him use it occasionally, especially for "thank you" notes. He was able to write his notes after his birthday with good success, and without practice and his writing was legible.

After the Lessons

What works for one child may not work for another. Working on Bubba's cursive was an ongoing process, and once he started back to school there was little time for the relaxed type of sessions we had over the summer. There were a long list of issues that needed worked on besides hand-writing and I felt we made good progress.

The teachers and the occupational therapist were shocked when Bubba returned to school. They really didn't think he could learn cursive. Unfortunately, once they discovered he was able to write cursive, they began trying to get him to write papers and long paragraphs in cursive and there was deterioration in the quality of his writing almost immediately. When I asked him why, he stated that he didn't have enough time. At that time, any hand-writing was somewhat laborious for Bubba, both cursive and print. I instructed Bubba not to write in cursive if he did not have enough time because I did not want his cursive to deteriorate in quality. As he got more practice in a no-pressure environment, his cursive quality stabilized.

I believe there is self-esteem tied to the ability to write in cursive, regardless of what I have been told, just like there is a gain in confidence with improvement in math and reading skills. I witnessed Bubba's confidence improve once he found he was able to write in cursive – even though he may not have been as fast or as eloquent as some other students. I also believe that leveraging Bubba's strengths, like his verbal processing skills and his willingness to commit to the process, while minimizing the time commitment, greatly contributed to his success.

I love my dog Bailey.

Writing Sample Years After Learning Cursive

In the sample above, Bubba jotted a cursive sample for me long after he graduated from high school. This sample was written years after Bubba spent a summer learning cursive. The lessons seemed to stick.

One Half of "L"

> *Perception of spatial relationships, ability to copy and draw geometric forms and designs, handwriting, reading comprehension, mathematics concepts and skills, and social perception and communication skills can be improved by explicit instruction.*[28]

An "e" is one half of "l" in cursive. It is half as tall. While teaching cursive writing to Bubba, I explained this only to be rewarded with a blank stare and an initial attempt at an "e" that looked pretty much like an "l". The concept or term "half as tall" did not make sense to him.

One day I lined up three pennies in a row on the kitchen countertop. I asked Bubba to make a row of pennies next to it that was twice as big as that row. I asked him to use pennies from a stack on the counter. He lined up three pennies next to my three pennies and then added two more to his row. This was somewhat perplexing to me, but consistent with other oddities I had noticed over time. The concept of "twice as big" just did not make any sense to him.

---

[28] Jean M. Foss, "Nonverbal Learning Disability: How to Recognize It and Minimize Its Effects," *ERIC Digests*, 2001.

It might sound like fractions or multiplication and I suppose it is, but "half as tall" and "twice as big" are verbal terms that express a size or magnitude relationship between two entities.

It also comes down to black and white. A rule is a rule. A lie is a lie. Generalizing didn't exist in Bubba's mind, only the specifics. Conversations were constantly derailed if details were slightly incorrect. There was no such thing as small slight by a peer. A slight was an insult and Bubba's responses became concerning. Razzing would result in a blow-up; indeed what seemed to be minor kid-stuff could result in Bubba extricating himself from a group, pouting and over-reacting.

I introduced him to insult levels and the school counselor supported the concept. He became familiar with the idea of a "Level 1," what was a harmless, joking statement or action. I came up with five levels:

- Level 1 – minor insult
- Level 2 – rudeness, on purpose
- Level 3 – rude, with physical threat
- Level 4 – physical action, on purpose, like hitting
- Level 5 – life-threatening event, like a gun to the head

I gave him examples of how guys can talk to each other and call each other jerks, and how that can actually be an odd sort of friendliness or a way of saying "Hi." Not something to get upset about and certainly not worthy of some of the responses he had been making.

What did insult levels have to do with an "e" being half of an "l"? I'm still not completely sure, but an "e" is a fraction of an "l". By carrying over the concept to human relationships, calling your buddy a "jerk" carries a fraction of the seriousness of having someone put a gun to your head. Indeed, "jerk" might not be an insult at all, but a friendly gesture.

The process of teaching cursive to Bubba had landed me into noticing deficits in Bubba's understanding of magnitude as well. Combined with a certain literalness I began to understand how these deficits subsequently affected his ability to interact socially.

Learning Measurements

> *Measurement of a quantity implies that a number is assigned to represent its magnitude. All other quantities are measured in units defined in relation to, or "derived" from, fundamental quantities.*[29]

"That building is at least ten inches tall!" or "He's four feet taller than I am." It was common for Bubba to express measures in units unrelated to an object of our discussion, or perhaps related to the discussion, but expressed using inappropriate units, or clearly off the mark. And this was in seventh grade. Another dilemma that needed addressing and would require some creativity.

The first measurements we tackled were inches, feet and yards. When I asked Bubba to show me how big an inch was, there was verbal fumbling, a few random gestures and a shrug of the shoulders. I had him hold up his hand and I had him find his pinky and his pinky knuckle. "Now, an inch is about as big as the last part of your finger here," I showed him. We got out the ruler and compared the knuckle to the ruler to see if the knuckle was about an inch.

---

[29] "Measurement" *The American Heritage Dictionary, Second College Edition* (Boston: Houghton Mifflin Company, 1976).

"So, how big is a foot?" I asked him. Again, there was verbal fumbling, random gestures and a shrug of the shoulders. "Hold up your foot," I told him. "That's about a foot." We measured the foot with a ruler to compare the sizes. I asked him then, how big was an inch, but he had already forgotten. So we reviewed these two concepts several times.

"So how big is a yard?" I asked him.

"As big as a yardstick," he replied. Okay, but I didn't give up there!

"It's about the distance from the floor up to your stomach," I told him. "Or, if you walk forward," and of course I had him stand and walk forward, "Put one foot down, the next right in front of it and then your third foot." Don't ask me why he understood this. "A yard is three feet," I told him.

"So how big is an inch?" I asked again. Of course he had already forgotten, so we reviewed again, and reviewed the foot concept and reviewed the yard concept. That constituted the first lesson. So you can see where we started in seventh grade.

Now, if I ask him how many inches are in a foot, how many feet in a yard, inches in a yard, inches in 5'11", ounces in a cup, cups in a pint, pounds in a ton, or any of the several similar questions, I get a straight and usually correct answer. This process from start to finish (is it ever really finished?) took about ten minutes a day, three or four days a week for about a month with frequent questions related to conversions using wrestler heights or some topic interesting to Bubba.

I created a checklist sheet with eleven questions regarding the measurements required in the seventh grade proficiency testing. On our first pass, he knew three or four of the answers. I had Bubba work through memorizing measurements. I repeated the questions periodically to check to see if he learned them, and then didn't forget them. An example of one of the checklist sheets is shown in the next figure.

Specially Educated

```
                                    8/6/08   9/8/08
                              12/16/08
  1. Inches in a foot? 12 *           ✓
  2. feet in a yard? 3    *           ✓
  3. inches in a yard? 36 *           ✓
  4. How many inches in 6'3"? 75"     ✓
  5. How many ounces in a cup? 8 *    ✓
  6. How many cups in a pint? 2 *     ✓
  7. How many quarts in a gallon? 4 * ✓
  8. How many days in a week? 7 *     ✓
  9. How many weeks in a year? DK *   ✓
 10. How many months in a year? 12 *
 11. How many days in a year? 365 *
```

Measurement Questions from Seventh Grade Standards

I began working on conversions with him, showing him the relationship mathematically between converting a small unit to a larger unit and vice versa. For example,

$$\text{Inches}/12 = \text{feet}$$
$$\text{Feet} * 12 = \text{inches}$$

An example of more work is shown in the next figure with conversions going back and forth between inches and feet. Repeated review of these types of questions with Bubba was helpful.

Specially Educated

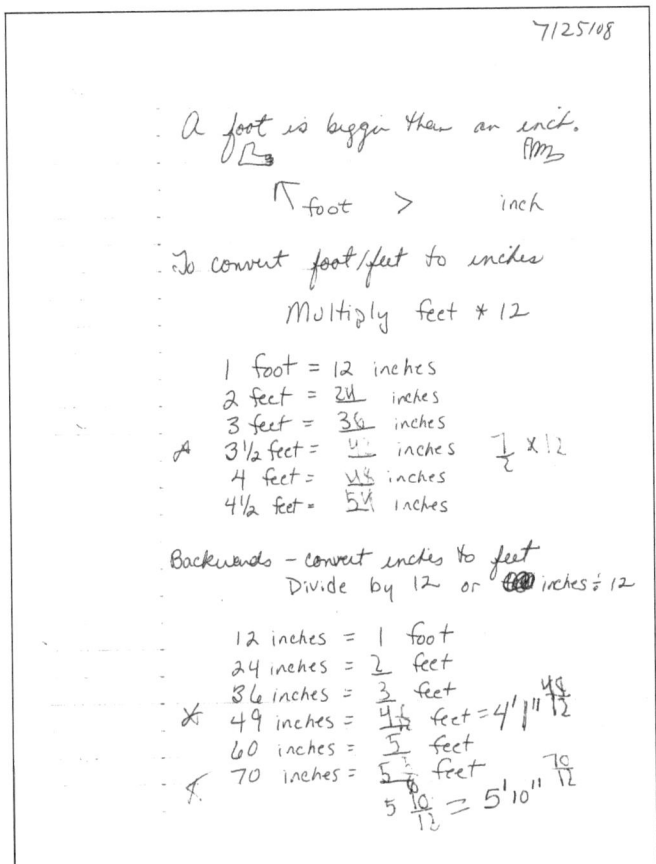

Examples of Feet to Inches and Inches to Feet

We added more cooking together, usually one day a week. That's about the extent of my patience. We looked at soda bottles, milk containers, and soup cans in the usual course of any day. We conversed about the size of the football field or miles to Grandma's house and worked on gasoline mileage calculations. There's no doubt in my mind that these measurement concepts needed to be instructed to Bubba, and should be taught to any child before he is qualified to enter high school, or eventually graduate from high school.

The problem however, was clearly in the forgetting. I had struggled to get measurements in Bubba's IEP at school and was told by the principal (future Assistant District Superintendent) that it was a "gap in the school district's curriculum and all the kids struggle." That didn't make me feel any better. My request to add measurements to the IEP was added and then dropped repeatedly until senior year when I apparently hit on a case manager who saw the same weakness and who, of course, had no knowledge of the district's previous refusals and forgetfulness. Finally, in the twelfth grade, measurements and conversions were added to Bubba's education plan, and they were worked on as part of targeted science tutoring. Better late than never, I suppose!

Learning Math

> *The goal for these students is to construct a strong verbal model for quantities and their relationships in place of the visual-spatial mental representation that most people develop. Consistent descriptive verbalizations also need to become firmly established in regard to when to apply math procedures and how to carry out the steps of written computation. Great patience and verbal repetition are required to make small incremental steps.*[30]

This is a short chapter because this is where I really got a break. A child who has visual-spatial deficits is one of the more challenging children to teach math, I am quite sure. By the time Bubba was in seventh grade, the school had been attempting to teach him two digit by two digit multiplication and division for three years. The same exact goals kept appearing in his IEP. Not good.

There were several problems that I noticed. Bubba would be taught and then forget what he had been taught. The teacher, perhaps overworked or frustrated, would hand out cluttered sheets of thirty or forty problems marked as wrong and the fun words, *"redo at home"* on the top of the

---

[30] Kate Garnett PhD, "Math Learning Disabilities," Division for Learning Disabilities, *Journal of the Council for Exceptional Children,* November, 1998.

page. These were my personal favorites. At the end of seventh grade, Bubba was still counting on his fingers.

On the other hand, he knew his multiplication tables early. I had set up a chart for him to use years earlier and then explained that division was the opposite of multiplication. For example, he knew six times four was twenty-four so it was easy to explain that twenty-four divided by six was four, and while addition and subtraction was very slow using the fingers, simple multiplication and division was strong. It led to me that he was doing better with the concepts taught at home.

I felt strongly that he needed to be monitored while working problems so that if he was doing a procedure improperly, it was stopped and corrected immediately, instead of repeating the wrong method thirty or forty times and solidly engraving it into Bubba's head. I can not express in words, completely, how the sinking feeling in my gut would emerge upon the receipt of class work stamped with the words *"redo at home."* The school's process for teaching math to Bubba was broken and ineffective. It would be a two or three day battle to convince Bubba he was doing his math problems incorrectly; then teach him the proper method; and then repeat it enough times that it would erase the improper method from his brain. We were wasting a lot of time.

I was seeing his standard scores plummet, compared to first and fourth grade, watching him falling farther and farther away from his peers' math skills, and indeed, even hearing the dreaded words "I'm stupid" accompanied by a visible loss of confidence. I finally hired a private tutor at the end of seventh grade. (By the way he was getting all A's and B's in math, oddly enough.) The tutor had been a teacher in India who didn't want to teach in the United States, but instead was studying for her database certification. We met her at the library, two or three days a week beginning that summer after seventh grade. He was testing at about a fourth grade level at that time.

"You try 'The Program' and you have no more math issue," she emphatically said one day after working with Bubba for about a month. [31] "He needs step-by-step, repetition." Skeptical, I was.

---

[31] "The Program" represents a specific after school, direct instruction methodology, math, reading and writing tutoring program that worked for Bubba.

Specially Educated

The next week we did check out the program she recommended and discussed whether Bubba could commit to the program. The instructor was very observant and asked Bubba if he had lost his confidence. I was shocked when he responded "Yes," and he did commit to the program. He really wanted to get better at math.

We attended the tutoring center once a week, but the bulk of the work was done at home. When he was being introduced to a new topic, I would work very closely with him to make sure he learned it correctly the first time. The program provided sufficient repetition so that the correct method was repeated over and over, and as I would see him consistently doing problems correctly, I would provide less and less assistance. In that math program, continual review of previously learned concepts was provided, so rarely did Bubba forget how to do a problem.

It was after two months or so that the counting on his fingers stopped. We fixed his problems with addition and subtraction; he breezed through multiplication and division; and Bubba went on to excel at fractions. What? That didn't seem possible, but within a year he was flying through his fractions. Within two years, he was successfully doing pre-algebra, and had progressed about four grade levels in his calculations. Still behind, but gaining!

Sounds like a break? Maybe not to some people – it might sound like a lot of work. But one of my Dad's favorite phrases comes to mind – "Do it right the first time or don't do it at all." Bubba could excel once he had his facts memorized and the correct process for each mathematical operation was learned. Repetition of the correct process was much more effective than repetition of the wrong process.

Statistical Note on Math Scores for Students with Disabilities

Math scores are lower for special education students – the average scaled score for all students ranged from 300 in 1978 to 306 in 2008 for the age 17 category. For the 17 year old with a disability, there were no scores in 1978, but the scaled scores were 277 in 2008. For 13-year olds with no disability, the math scaled scores ranged from 264 in 1978 to 281 in 2008. Similarly, there were no scores for 1978 for 13-year olds with a disability, but their scaled scores in 2008 were 246.

Middle school math for special education students taking regular assessments - The average rate of proficiency in math for students with disabilities in middle school increased from 18% in 2001-2002 to 22% in 2004-2005.

High school math for special education students taking regular assessments - In 2001-2002, the 24 states in the report had an average rate of 23% of students with disabilities who were proficient and above on regular assessments in math; that rate was 22% in 2004-2005.[32]

---

[32] National Center on Educational Outcomes, "Trends in the Participation and Performance of Students with Disabilities," *Technical Report 50*, July 2008.

The Aides

An Aide???-- or ... an Executive Assistant for their Executive Dysfunction![33]

The first year Bubba was given an aide was in eighth grade. Bubba was supposed to be getting tutoring for language arts class, specifically for his writing skills, but the school district forgot what was agreed on in mediation and gave Bubba an aide instead. (The mediation is described in Part 3.) I thought he was getting tutoring but eventually discovered that tutoring wasn't being provided. The aide was their version of a tutor and was added without our (the parents) permission. An aide and a tutor are not the same thing, at least not in my opinion.

The law governing special education services (*IDEA*) does not mention the term aide or tutor directly. There are references to paraprofessionals which are "appropriately and adequately prepared and trained, including that those personnel have the content knowledge and skills to serve children with disabilities." Under the law, an aide or tutor would provide special education under the guidance of the special education teacher.

---

[33] Dr. Dean Mooney, Workshop proceedings on "Nonverbal Learning Disabilities," Maple Leaf Clinic, 2006.

When the district provided an aide, they provided Bubba and other special education children in the general education classroom a person who would "keep them on track." This person did not provide one-on-one tutoring to remediate Bubba's writing skills. As part of the mediation process, we had "one-on-one tutoring" written into Bubba's IEP. The district did not follow the IEP, and in hindsight trying to prove that an aide was not a tutor would have been difficult because of the vagueness in the definitions of tutor and aide.

I wouldn't have known about the aide except that Bubba mentioned her name several times during our conversations about school. I asked him who she was and that's when I discovered that there was an aide. Apparently the district thought that if Bubba were to be removed from the resource room, he should have an aide. I'm sure there was no analysis to determine that, and there certainly wasn't a discussion with us, the parents. The IEP listed a set number of minutes of one-on-one tutoring for writing and the substitution of an aide to keep the special education students on track was not providing that service.

Indeed, the aide only seemed to piss Bubba off. Sometime later in the eighth grade year I caught wind of another player on the scene because Bubba began mentioning another person's name.

"Who is that?" I asked him.

"My new aide," he replied. He hadn't been getting along too well with the first aide.

The function of the aide(s) in eighth grade seemed vague to me. From what I could gather the aide helped Bubba take his tests and organize papers in his various binders.[34]

---

[34] Note: The aide always wrote her notes and directions for Bubba in cursive – the very writing form the district insisted he would never need to use because "everything is on the computer now" and it wasn't necessary. If I hadn't taught him how to write and read cursive he would never have been able to even understand the aide's directions! If he couldn't write or read the cursive how was he supposed to utilize the aide's assistance? Not only that, many of his teachers naturally wrote in cursive, so it was astonishing to me that they would declare it unimportant. How much information was Bubba not able to understand prior to learning cursive, just because he was unable to read the instructor's handwriting?

One day Bubba described how he took his science test. "I go to a separate room to take my tests," he told me.

"Is anyone else there?" I inquired.

"The aide," he stated.

"What does she do?"

"She reads the questions to me."

"Can't you read them?"

Bubba got disgusted with me then. I could tell. He gave me one of those looks. "Yes, I can read them." Duh!

"So what is the aide for?" I pressed on.

"If I answer a question wrong, she makes me go back and redo the question," he answered matter-of-factly. "If my answer isn't right then we look at the other answers for a better one."

"Does she tell the answers?" I asked. I didn't feel real positive about the assistance of the aide at this point. I would have liked to have a video recording of their interchanges. I am sure it would have been fascinating.

"She just helps me get the right answers." Even Bubba didn't appear too comfortable with the process.

I found this appalling. My approach had been to find ways to teach Bubba how to do tests on his own. With many activities and areas that needed work, it was often the easy way out to do things for him and sometimes with time constraints, I know I was guilty of that also. The aide seemed to be a person assisting Bubba with getting better grades, but not with helping Bubba learn how to get better grades himself.

Confronting District Coordinator 3 (because by this time Number 2 was long gone) did no good either because her response was predictable, saying, "That is certainly not what an aide does!"

Sometime around November of freshman year I caught wind of an aide again. (This could have been in an email.) Similar to eighth grade, an aide had been assigned without our knowledge, and an aide wasn't in Bubba's IEP. The aide was present in Bubba's language arts class where they were doing a lot of map quizzes.

Bubba hadn't been doing too well on his map quizzes, typically scoring two or three correct out of twenty or so questions. As I looked through his papers one night, I found a map quiz from that day which was scored 38 out of 38. Perfect! A miracle?

"Bubba, come here," I yelled. Bubba came downstairs to the living room where I showed him the perfect quiz. "What is this?"

"That was our big quiz today."

"How did you get them all right?" I asked. I couldn't help but be a little suspicious. I am an analyst.

"The aide let me keep the map with the answers out and just copy the answers onto the quiz," he stated.

It was shortly after this revelation that we started studying maps using a more visual-sequential method (see Maps and Data). Instead of finding a way to teach Bubba how to read maps so he could get a better grade himself, the aide simply set the answers in front of him so he could copy them and get a good grade. I understood that she was probably concerned about Bubba's growing frustration and did not know how to handle the situation.

Giving him the answers was not the method I had in mind though.

I suppose it is possible that this instance and the other instance were the only two times that aides were simply boosting Bubba's grades. But I doubt it. Fortunately, by tenth grade Bubba was freed from all aides and the resource room. He was left to function on his own and he was a lot less pissed off.

Teacher Meetings

> *"Our midterm and final exams never leave our classroom (this is common policy for Social Studies and English classes). If you would like to make an appointment between 7 AM and 2:45 PM to come in and go through the questions, we would be happy to make the test available to you in our classroom."*[35]

Throughout Bubba's career in the public education system, I made a concerted attempt to attend the teacher's meetings. They were usually about two or three months into the school year (held in the evening by appointment, but at least they didn't require taking unpaid leave during the workday) and I looked forward to them almost as much as I looked forward to the IEP team meetings.

In elementary school the meeting usually consisted of meeting with the special education teacher and, perhaps the occupational therapist. Everything is small in elementary school. When I attended those meetings I was always sitting in a very small chair, feeling very small.

I clearly remember the teacher meeting in eighth grade. At this event, there was a circle of student desks placed at one end of the literature

---

[35] Response from English teacher to Ex's email wanting to help Bubba review an English test.

teacher's classroom. They were not the little chairs I had to sit on during the elementary meetings; these were the desks that allowed you to slip in from the left side and do your writing on the right side – an attached chair/desk contraption (none too convenient for the lefty, I might add).

So there they were – the literature teacher, an older woman with grey hair done up in a bun, the history teacher, a red-faced action-oriented looking man, the science teacher and the special education teacher. I came in carrying Bubba's binder.

The special education teacher opened with the usual pleasantries and introductions. I got straight to the point as there were only fifteen minutes allowed, and how on earth could we cover all the issues in that amount of time? So I stood up and opened Bubba's binder. Papers flew across the half-desk, onto the wooden attached chair and all over the floor.

"I think we have an organization problem," I said. That served as the topic for the next fifteen minutes.

The teacher meetings never really got much better. Each year I asked the same questions and was handed grade sheets that I had already seen. Many of the meetings involved discussions about some classroom behavior that Bubba exhibited that either confused or bothered the teacher. Occasionally I was told what a nice boy Bubba was and how he liked to participate and ask questions. Those types of comments at least made me feel a little better because I felt it was evidence he was becoming more confident. I usually received several suggestions for activities I could be working on at home with Bubba (like I didn't already excel in that area).

During the summer before ninth grade there were a series of scheduling conflicts that had to be addressed. We frequently seemed to have scheduling conflicts. I hadn't met any of Bubba's high school teachers yet but I had a series of telephone and email exchanges with his new case manager/homeroom teacher.

Apparently the classes that we selected at the end of eighth grade were generating a scheduling problem for the case manager. Ex and I were insisting that Bubba be in physical education the entire year and wanted him enrolled in the swimming class. The case manager was finding it difficult to schedule swimming and keep the resource room in Bubba's schedule.

"I already told Bubba he would get the swimming and when I told him it wasn't in his schedule anymore he started to cry." I blatantly lied to the case manager.

The case manager was trying to schedule Bubba into resource room classes for math and science and the regular classroom for history and English, and it just wasn't possible to complete that schedule and incorporate swimming class. Finally after listening to my pathetic pleading, he sent a revised schedule and notified me that if Bubba was going to be in swimming he would have to be moved out of the resource room for all classes. I couldn't have been more pleased.

As I indicated before, the system is not a single-brained organism that magically remembers what decisions it has previously made. While we had fought to get Bubba out of the resource room for eighth grade reading, and were advised that it was only temporary, the temporary part was forgotten by the bureaucratic brain. Indeed, while we remembered the struggle, the new case manager naively moved Bubba out of the resource room for all classes.

By the time I met Bubba's case manager in ninth grade, I felt like we had known each other a long time. It took almost a month, several calls and a lot of emails to finally resolve the schedule.

Of course that wasn't the end of the emails. As ninth grade rolled on and prior to the teacher meetings, we had a flurry of high-technology messaging as the new set of teachers were broken in. Bubba was taking an English/Humanities class that brought many kids to tears. The class seemed to be a kind of educational hazing designed to stun the young high schoolers into submission by piling hours of useless homework on them each evening, weekend and holiday break.

Later in the year, the students would be required to generate around 1000 3x5 index cards as preparation for their research paper in that class. I am talking pure torture.

Apparently Bubba's organizational skills needed more work. I received the following message early in the year from the case manager. This was only one of about a hundred I received in the first three months of high school, many with a similar tone.

> *I just spoke with Bubba's Humanities teachers and he (and his teachers) had some frustrations today in class. Students are starting to write papers in class. Apparently Bubba could not find his and when it was finally found it was only half finished. This has to be completed in order to write the next two paragraphs (this is step 1 and 2 on the worksheet below) which is tonight's homework. So tonight he needs to work on these three things. He also was missing the in-class paragraph that was written on the board last week. He could not find this/did not copy it down off of the board. I will have one of the other students give me a copy of theirs tomorrow in class and I will make a copy of it for him.*
>
> *I guess Bubba became frustrated during class as well as did his teachers as they had to spend the majority of the time with him just looking for his chart and paragraphs. This obviously took away from his teachers being able to help any other students. I would imagine Bubba was frustrated because he felt their frustration. I am not sure if we need to look at his binder to see if it is unorganized (?). When I looked at it the other day it looked pretty good. Or did he not understand what to get out for class (?). Or did he know what was asked to be taken out but knew it was not finished (?). High School Coordinator has put another aide in the class to help Bubba, but I am not sure if this person is a sub-aide or a permanent aide. I am cc'ing this to him to find out. In the meantime I will talk with Bubba tomorrow to see what might have been wrong and see where he is with this assignment. Any help you could provide at home to help catch him up would be appreciated.*

We had a lot to talk about in the teacher meetings in ninth grade and I didn't even have to pull out his binder.

Maps and Data

Different modes of spatial thinking make use of different brain structures that operate in parallel – that is simultaneously rather than sequentially. In other words, there is no "natural" sequence that students should follow in applying spatial-thinking skills to a specific problem. There are significant differences among students in their predisposition to use particular modes of spatial thinking to address a problem.[36]

This is the email I received in the winter of ninth grade from Bubba's case manager.

"Just wanted to give you a 'heads up' on something that happened today with Bubba. I would normally call, but I was not sure if I would be able to reach both of you so I apologize for giving the info in an e-mail. If you would like me to call you just let me know and I will try to as soon as possible.

Today during study center Bubba came in and immediately put his head down. I asked him what was going on and he kept telling me nothing. I had a feeling he was upset and I could see

---

[36] Teachers Guide, "Project GeoSTART: Geo-Spatial Thinking Activities and Resources for Teachers of Geography and Earth Science," Association of American Geographers, 2008.

it in his face. A few minutes later I noticed him hitting himself in the head. I immediately asked him to come out in the hall as I did not want any of the other students to see him doing this and thus make a comment. As he came close to me he was starting to cry. I talked with him in the hall and he was telling me how he was not good at anything he tries to do. After talking to him I was able to get to the bottom of the problem which was he did not do well on his Humanities quizzes. I asked him why he thought he did not do well and he said he did not know."

I was able to question Bubba about the incident when he came home and finally wrangled the truth out of him. It was the maps. Each week the ninth grade literature and history class (Humanities) was required to study a map of ancient Babylonia, or ancient Europe, or modern day Europe. Bubba was repeatedly getting two or three questions right per twenty questions or so (except for when the aide let him copy all the correct answers), and not feeling very good about it.

One set of data I had was related to his visual therapy we did at home with the help of the pediatric optometrists at the State University. This was a visual battery of tests that they performed before and after the visual therapy. Of course I liked that they measured before and after. Bubba had made good gains in an area called "visual sequential," but was still low in the "visual organization" area.

Shortly after the "map" email, we headed off to San Francisco for a long weekend to go whale watching and meet up with friends. As we took off over the city, Bubba pointed out the window at various landmarks in the city sequentially as we passed over them.

It was about a week later, as I determinedly pursued a remedy for his troubles, that it occurred to me (as I was running on the treadmill, of course) that maybe instead of trying to study the maps in the traditional way (whatever that is), he could learn them similar to how we flew over the city. He could "fly" in from the east and locate landmarks along the way.

We tried the process at home. Bubba added one letter cheats (a letter representing each location) to the process so that he could remember strings of locations that ran north and south perpendicular to the east to west flying path. He began getting seventeen or eighteen right out of twenty or so questions and stopped hitting himself in the head (at least for a while).

The normal scores on visual sequential versus the visual organization were the key. When I explained the event to NeuroPsych he said, "That makes sense. He is using his visual sequential skills where he is stronger instead of the visual organization skills that are weaker." I tried explaining that to Bubba's case manager who just said "Huh," and I didn't bother trying to explain it to the aide. (See the chapter on "The Aides" for a more complete explanation of my reasoning.) NeuroPsych understood the logic behind the method, which at least helped validate the approach. That and the fact that Bubba started passing his map quizzes on his own.

Special Games and Activities

> *The mistake is thinking that achievement is a by-product of high self-esteem. It is more likely that self-esteem is a product of rising achievement and meaningful accomplishments, not a means by which to attain knowledge and skills.*[37]

There are a variety of games we invented along the way to help teach concepts that are just plain boring to talk about or to enforce academics, help social skills or just understand what people are talking about.

"What do you do when ..."

This was an easy game Bubba and I played during dinner or while out walking around the neighborhood. The first person made up a situation, such as "You are in math class and cut a fart. What do you do?" Or, "A new kid at school looks lost in the hallway. What do you do?" We also called this game "Dilemma."

---

[37] William L. Heward, "Ten Faulty Notions About Teaching and Learning That Hinder the Effectiveness of Special Education," *The Journal of Special Education*, 36 (4), 2003.

Specially Educated

Waiting Rooms

For waiting rooms, there was nothing more fun for a vocabulary fanatic then running through the alphabet thinking of words that start with a letter. Bubba liked big words so this could get crazy. If we stumbled on a tricky word, I challenged him to spell it. For a variation, we played last letter, where one person starts their word with the last letter of the other person's word. We even got NeuroPsych involved in this game and he liked it.

Math Games

Math was not math when it was wrestling or *Pokemon*, or whatever Bubba was obsessed with at any particular time. He learned a lot of math playing *Yugi-Oh*. We spent some time designing a casket for a *World Wrestling Entertainment* wrestler (this was a three-dimensional rectangular shape), then calculated how much carpet it would take to cover the casket, and how much water it would take to fill it up. Likewise, converting feet to inches is not math when it pertained to a 7'2" wrestler.

Quiz Mom

Getting Bubba to study independently was always a challenge, and quizzing him could turn into a battle. However, quizzing Mom was really fun because she didn't know all the answers!

The Maid Did It

Making a bed or cleaning a bathroom is stupid. But if the maid did it, Mom got really surprised and confused. Bubba would maintain a deadpan expression (with barely a hint of smile) when I would check his bedroom and he would tell me that "the maid did it," referring to a clean room or a made-up bed. I would respond with disbelief and complain that the maid didn't make my bed. That was fun.

Who Is It?

The *Who Is It* game was a take-off on charades. We played it a lot when out on walks where we would imitate someone we knew. The other person had to guess who was being imitated. Sometimes we enforced the "no talking" rule. For a child who supposedly was not observant of non-verbal information, facial expressions and their meanings, Bubba actually was very observant of people and their idiosyncrasies.

Expressions

Imagine interpreting everything literally. Run to the store, pain in the neck, drop the bomb, and miss the boat. In this game, one person picked a word and the other person had to provide a common expression that used the word. I found that Bubba began asking a lot more questions about expressions after we played this game. It really made me wonder how much confusion he had experienced his entire life, considering that some people (including teachers, parents, and coaches) used a lot of expressions. Even some tests and many books use common expressions that most of us might infer meaning from, but for a youngster who takes expressions literally, the meaning may be entirely different from what was intended.

Facial Expressions and Body Language

This was another game we would play when out walking (it sounds like we walked a lot) where one person named an emotion and the other person demonstrated it with the face or with body movement (no talking, of course). Or reverse the game, where one person demonstrated the emotion and the other person guessed it.

Marine Biology Year

At the beginning of ninth grade, as Bubba was beginning to gain academically and his confidence began improving, I felt that we should get out more. I decided a theme for that year would be an interesting way to determine activities, and since Bubba had declared that he was interested in marine biology, it became "Marine Biology Year." We visited several aquariums during the year in places such as San Francisco and Cincinnati. We flew to the Florida Keys where Bubba was "Dolphin Trainer for a Day" and we dined on the waterfront in the evening. This was a big confidence builder. We also went whale watching in Half Moon Bay, near San Francisco, and spent a good part of the day out on the Pacific Ocean. Having a theme provided fun and continuity to the activities.

Visual Therapy

In eighth grade we began visiting the State University to have extensive testing performed for normal vision ability, but also for a complete evaluation of how well the eyes were working together. He was diagnosed as having convergence insufficiency and an astigmatism in both eyes. In combination with some activities at the University and a pair of special glasses, Bubba participated in a computer-based visual therapy program at home. This took about six months to complete and improved some of the visual performance measures, particularly visual sequential memory, or the ability to remember characters, letters or shapes in the correct sequentially presented order.

Tennis

After years of different sports, it had become apparent to me that I needed a better strategy than the recreation leagues. By the end of eighth grade, there were very few leagues for the older kids. I asked Bubba to pick a sport to participate in at the beginning of ninth grade and he selected tennis. Not sure what to do, I signed him up for one-on-one lessons. The instructor suggested Bubba get involved in the group lessons, but I held off on that idea for about nine months and let him have the private instruction. It gave him time to build up his skill-set and then merge into the group lessons with confidence. I can't say enough about how good the tennis was for Bubba in terms of improving his balance, footwork, eye-hand coordination, and good sportsmanship. He also has a game for life that he can play.

Camps, Religion and Volunteering

Religion is one of the most important and beneficial activities in Bubba's life. However abnormal things may have gotten at school, Bubba's interactions with the other kids at religious functions were a breath of fresh air. He spoke like an eloquent, young man at his Bar Mitzvah, he spoke engagingly again at his confirmation, he attended activities sponsored by the Temple, and they were fairly normal, even encouraging at times, and even inspiring on a couple of occasions.

By the end of ninth grade, Bubba was suggesting that he attend a religious camp out of state for a month. This camp was 250 miles away from home, in the woods with no telephone and no computer connections. I was supposed to drop him off there with a month's worth of clothes and come back a month later and pick him up. I did, but only because it was a structured, religious-based camp.

But not so structured that the kids wouldn't get really dirty and have a ton of fun. When I returned to pick him up after a month, he was wearing flip-flops, stinky, moldy clothes, a large smile and a camper on each arm. It was another big boost to his confidence and an opportunity for me to spend large amounts of time at home plotting an educational strategy and staring at the ceiling. After he returned home from camp, he spent the remainder of the summer volunteering at the Temple organizing their basement and filling out job applications, mostly for practice, as he was still fifteen.

The summer after tenth grade was another opportunity for more volunteering and a different type of camp. He was also very interested in video games, so he attended a camp where the campers developed video games and were able to bring their creations home and play them. This gave him an opportunity to try the business out, in a sense, as he was hoping to make his career in the video game field. He volunteered at the library as well and again, filled out job applications. It required some pushing and assistance on my part, but he was beginning to get the hang of it, and the practice sure didn't hurt.

He returned to the video game development camp the next summer as well, the summer before his senior year. He incorporated that work into his senior project. One week of that camp he lived on-campus, in the dorms. It gave him a sense of what living away from home might be like and helped me as well, because it was another baby-step towards his independence.

Cooking

Here is a skill that is good for anyone to learn. What I had to remember was to not jump in and to let Bubba read the directions, measure ingredients, and basically manhandle the kitchen. By high school, I felt comfortable that during the summer he could make his own lunch and I didn't need to worry about fires or explosions while I was at work (not much worrying anyway).

Summary

Special games and activities was about taking baby steps, thinking outside the box, and approaching typical activities as learning experiences, all the while keeping my fingers crossed. Most of the activities are great for any child; it just sometimes took a lot more patience, or perhaps some modifications. The visual therapy and games related to facial expressions and literalness were important and specific to Bubba's unique character. I incorporated them with the purpose of helping him make sense of concepts that did not come naturally to him.

Five IEP Meetings and an Expert

> *The public agency must ensure that the IEP Team for each child with a disability includes -- the parents of the child...*[38]

After so many meetings with the IEP teams, I had become used to misunderstandings. Each year started over with a new team that had no experience with a kid like Bubba. Each year Bubba got a new case manager, the primary special education teacher that served as the primary parent contact for the student. The case manager also served as the special education representative in every IEP team meeting. For some reason it was common for one of Bubba's teachers to complain about some aspect of Bubba's behavior in every meeting. I was used to it.

Bubba was still having his ups and downs in ninth grade. His English teacher, who was serving as the general education classroom teacher for IEP purposes, started the first IEP meeting off that year with the statement, "He always puts his head down in my class."

"So in the last 20 days of attending class, how many of those days has he put his head down," I asked.

---

[38] See 34 CFR 300.321 (a)

I got the look from her, believe me. She hesitated and then responded, "About two or three times."

"That's about 10% of the time," I commented. "That doesn't sound like always." I wasn't sure what this had to do with anything as he learned better with his ears anyway. "Deal with it," I said. Okay, probably not the most diplomatic comment but I thought there were a lot more disruptive activities a student could engage in that she could complain about.

High School Director excused the general education classroom teacher from her IEP duties after our interchange because she needed to get back to class. (Note that this is a technical violation of *IDEA*, and was quite common at Bubba's school. Well it used to be anyway.) We asked about adding the writing tutoring using "The Program" because it was working so well for Bubba's math, and High School Director commented, "If you find something that works, stick with it." I was surprised because this was actually a very logical reply, something I was not used to. (Actually, his response was a violation as well, because he should have provided Prior Written Notice that they were not going to provide a requested service.)

All in all, this first IEP meeting was a short one. There was no mention of resource room in the IEP anywhere for the first time in Bubba's educational career. While Ex and I were there, we signed the IEP promptly, knowing that in order for the district to move Bubba back into the resource room they would need our signature or would need to take us to Due Process. For that reason, we decided to run with the signed IEP and address the tutoring after the meeting.

This was the first of five IEP meetings in ninth grade, four of which were spent blocking the district's attempts to move Bubba back into the resource room because they claimed that it was the only way that they could provide writing tutoring. I had already enrolled him in "The Program" for additional reading and writing tutoring (in addition to the math tutoring), taking High School Director's advice.

It was shortly after this meeting that I filed my first Formal Complaint with the State Department of Education. I expressed my concerns in the complaint regarding the lack of math and writing tutoring. In hopes of resolving the complaint the district suggested that we have another IEP meeting. I suggested they get an independent expert to evaluate the need for tutoring and then have another IEP meeting.

Shortly after this suggestion, an independent expert arrived and was directed by the district to evaluate Bubba and his need for writing tutoring. She performed the evaluation and we asked to see a copy of her recommendations a week before the IEP meeting so we could digest her comments.

We still hadn't seen a copy of her report the day before the IEP meeting so I emailed District Coordinator 3 that we would need to reschedule the meeting. I found out the next day that the district held the IEP meeting, even though Ex and I were not present and still had not seen the results of the independent evaluator. Needless to say, I was livid.

The district even drafted up a new IEP during that meeting where we were not in attendance. Note that we had never missed an IEP meeting. Ever! The new IEP suggested that writing tutoring using a direct instruction method be added to Bubba's IEP, according to the recommendations of the expert, and in order to facilitate the service, Bubba would need to be moved back into the resource room. The district completely ignored our requests for an evaluation of the need for math tutoring (another violation).

I requested they send me a copy of the meeting minutes so I could see what was discussed in our absence. As I read through the minutes I noticed that one of the teachers had commented on how effective "The Program" had been for Bubba's math skills. I wonder what else was said when I was not around?

It took three more IEP meetings before we could finally agree on an IEP that did not move Bubba into the resource room and still had the writing tutoring included. Because the district had not incorporated the math tutoring (this was directed in the previous year's IEP and they had neglected to provide the service), I was hesitant to sign the IEP. What I finally did, was sign the IEP that I agreed with the changes to add the writing tutoring. Then I wrote on the back of the IEP my issues regarding the sections that I disagreed with – specifically the lack of math tutoring.

The Writing Tutor

> *It is the teacher who is disabled in a classroom where children are not writing creatively – not the children.*[39]

After five IEP meetings in ninth grade, the school district finally agreed to provide writing tutoring for Bubba beginning in the final quarter of the school year. This tutoring agreement was subsequent to the previous agreement in eighth grade that we negotiated during the mediation where the district and parents agreed Bubba *needed* tutoring in both writing and math. Remember, they forgot to provide the tutoring in eighth grade, but I hadn't forgotten at all.

So finally they acquiesced after I pounded them with a complaint to the State Department of Education. The school district's expert had recommended three possible tutoring programs that were based on the principles of direct instruction, a methodology that provides scripted lesson plans so there is a minimum amount of interpretation necessary. This reduces the chances of miscommunication due to different interpretations of the material. One-on-one oversight with immediate feedback and correction is another component of direct instruction and this was the methodology used in "The Program" as well.

---

[39] Harlow G. Unger, *The Learning Disabilities Trap, How to Save Your Child from the Perils of Special Education* (Chicago: Contemporary Books, 1997).

The district had the required manuals for one of the programs in-house but hadn't actually used the materials yet.

"So, you are using Bubba as a guinea pig?" I asked. I suppose I wasn't always the easiest parent to deal with. We had the previous experience in eighth grade with the computer-based math program they attempted to use with Bubba. (See Data, Bad Data and Useless Data in Part 3.) They had no experience using that program either, used Bubba as a guinea pig, and it turned out to be a huge failure. I wasn't that optimistic.

District Coordinator 3 (the consultant) assured me that the district could successfully implement the program. (Please note that was the last I ever saw of the consultant; she quickly retired at the end of that school year to go live on the lake.) We agreed that the tutoring would take place two to three times per week for 25 minutes per session. Indeed, the district planned to use an aide to provide the tutoring, a woman who did have an English degree but no teaching degree, and who had never used or been trained on the direct instruction program the district decided to implement.

I wasn't exactly keen on having another aide involved in Bubba's education program.

Given that the district had a less-than-stellar history of performing the services that were agreed on and written into Bubba's IEP, I had a certain amount of skepticism that Bubba would ever get any tutoring from the district. Naturally, since I had already enrolled him in the reading and writing portion of "The Program" six months earlier (sometime right after IEP meeting #1 that year), I kept him enrolled, just in case.

As the last quarter of ninth grade began and when the district's writing tutoring was supposed to begin, I decided to post a chart on the refrigerator to track their schedule. When Bubba came home from school, I would ask him whether he received any writing tutoring that day and post the date if the tutoring happened. Of course there were various sessions missed due to special circumstances.

It seemed to be progressing well. That made me somewhat suspicious – it sounded too good to be true! By the third week, I got smarter. I began requesting more detail from Bubba.

"Did you have your writing tutoring today?" I asked one Monday.

"Yes."

"What did you do there?" I asked.

"Mrs. Aide had me type on the computer," Bubba replied.

"Didn't you use the District Program?" I asked. (I am using the term District Program to refer to their direct instruction program they decided to use.) I started to sense that the district was deviating from our agreement again. They were supposed to be using preplanned, scripted lessons that were followed sequentially using a workbook that came with the program materials. One of us read the instructions.

"No, she had me type this on the computer and then she had to help some other kids." Bubba held of a piece of paper with several words typed on it.

"What is this?"

"That is what she told me to type," Bubba stated. The results of that particular 25-minute writing direct instruction tutoring session are shown in the next figure.

```
Where:

When:

Action Verbs:

Introduce Characters:

Dialogue:
```

Sample of Writing Tutoring – Bubba Types Five Categories

Specially Educated

The sample from the school district's writing tutoring session shows exactly what was accomplished in the 25 minutes. Bubba had successfully typed five categories onto a sheet of paper and sat at the computer for the remainder of the period. There is no relationship of this assignment to any of the scripted lessons in the direct instruction program. None of the categories were started, drafted or brainstormed. Just five category items typed on a page in the 25-minute lesson.

As the quarter progressed, what should have been 18 sessions, amounted to about 10 or so, only one of which used the direct instruction materials we agreed would be used. It took me two months to get the data and copies of the 10 session outputs from the school district. I filed copies of the data with a series of complaints that summer. The State Department of Education determined that the district had kept their part of the bargain in providing the tutoring as required in Bubba's IEP. They denied there was any action required by the complaint (on that issue). I think Bubba got seriously cheated.

The district didn't bother continuing the program (that they weren't providing) when school began the next fall either – big surprise. Fortunately, Bubba was still enrolled in "The Program," which was a direct instruction program, where he continued to jump several grade levels in reading and writing while he was enrolled.

NeuroPsych Returns

> *Start with a good, child neuropsychologist...That assessment is key.*[40]

In ninth grade I suggested several times, both verbally and in writing, that Bubba be evaluated by NeuroPsych for his upcoming evaluation. He was due for his three-year evaluation to determine whether or not he needed special education. The school district ignored my request, which was again, *in writing,* and told me verbally that they could evaluate him.

That summer I took him to NeuroPsych and paid for it out of pocket, because the last time the school district performed an evaluation on Bubba they had incorrectly characterized his issues. I took Bubba to the same neuropsychologist he saw in seventh grade. Again the process took about three days and included subjective input from Bubba's former teachers.

When I met with NeuroPsych after he had completed his evaluation, he commented on the incredible improvements he noticed with Bubba. I

---

[40] Rondalyn V. Whitney, *Bridging the Gap: Raising a Child with Nonverbal Learning Disorder* (New York: The Berkley Publishing Group, 2002).

had informed him about the out-of-school program and he documented the effectiveness of "The Program" in his report. He also commented verbally that the school district certainly would not want to add "The Program" to Bubba's IEP because it would set a precedent.

In the fall of tenth grade, NeuroPsych came back to the school and presented the results from the evaluation he performed over the summer. I dedicated myself to taking minutes during the meeting, because by this time, I was getting everything in writing. I would type up the minutes of any meeting and send the IEP team a copy requesting that they "make note of any inaccuracies in the minutes." This is one way to document meetings and get comments and requests in writing.

From the minutes:

> *NeuroPsych found Bubba socially intact and cautioned to watch for anxiety. He suggested extra time for tests and oral retesting. He noted that Bubba wants to do well and be in the regular education class. He expects Bubba to struggle with maps, geography and math, particularly word problems, physics and geometry. He noted that "The Program" had improved Bubba's math. He noted that Bubba would have difficulty with visual cues, tone of voice and social interpretation.*

It was fortunate that I took minutes at the meeting because (no surprise here) District Coordinator 4 conveniently forgot that NeuroPsych had specifically commented on the effectiveness of "The Program." By this time I had figured out that she would routinely and conveniently forget many things, thus the note taking and forwarding minutes back to the team.

After the meeting, District Coordinator 4 wanted a copy of the neuropsychological report. She had assumed that they could use the report for the school district's required three-year reevaluation. This was sensible because they would have to perform their own evaluation by an overworked staff, a staff that had lesser qualifications. She asked NeuroPsych for a copy, but he deferred her to me.

I told her they could have a copy but they would need to pay for it. This prompted District Coordinator 4 to contact Assistant District Superintendent, because now it was a financial issue. I reminded them both that they had ignored my written requests for a neuropsychological reevaluation the previous year and had not provided me with Prior Written Notice, or a reason for denying my request. Now they wanted the report and I felt they should pay for it. They did pay for it and used it in place of the evaluation they were required to perform. That was just fine with me.

Learning a Foreign Language

"High school students who studied a foreign language consistently scored higher on ACT English and mathematics components than did students who did not study a foreign language in high school."[41]

"Bubba won't be able to learn a foreign language. We just don't think he should take a foreign language in high school." This was the input from the teachers at our last meeting in middle school before Bubba moved on to high school. We were reviewing his schedule for ninth grade and this was the same spiel we were given when Bubba had the opportunity to take a foreign language in middle school.

I remember thinking it odd that he had just gone through his Bar-Mitzvah where he was required to read and speak in Hebrew. Wasn't that a foreign language? I couldn't understand Hebrew myself, but I knew it couldn't be easy as it was composed of complicated symbols and text that was read backwards.

---

[41] S.A. Olsen and L.K. Brown, "The Relation Between High School Study of Foreign Languages and ACT English and Mathematics Performance," ADFL Bulletin, 23(3), from ERIC Database, 1992.

I conceded that Bubba taking a foreign language in the ninth grade was probably not a good idea. I was immersed in difficulty with the school district at that time and losing trust rapidly, but did not want to pursue the matter because I knew transitioning to high school could be a rough time for Bubba. I didn't want to add a subject that might add too much stress (this turned out to be a very wise choice).

The subject of foreign language came up again almost two years later as I was involved in putting together Bubba's schedule for eleventh grade. This meeting was with his tenth grade case manager, a very nice fellow who had no idea of the discussions that ensued at Bubba's middle school or in the planning of his ninth grade schedule. Indeed, Bubba was doing fairly well in tenth grade and gaining independence and confidence.

"Next year there will be algebra II, English, chemistry and European history. Bubba will need to pick electives as well and I was thinking he should take a foreign language. A lot of colleges expect students to have taken at least two years," the case manager explained. I had learned by this time not to volunteer too much information about what I had been told in the past. What he was telling me sounded like the thinking of a reasonable man.

"What are the options?" I asked. I wasn't about to clue him in that a prior team had declared foreign language as a no-no.

"Well, there is Spanish, German or French."

"Okay. I'll talk it over with Bubba and make sure he signs up for a foreign language next year." That evening when I discussed it with Bubba, he declared that he wanted to learn German. I wasn't sure exactly how useful German would be and I didn't speak a lick of German. I convinced him to go with Spanish (primarily because there was a lot of Spanish seen in every day life and I was somewhat familiar with it) and so he enrolled in Spanish for his eleventh grade year.

Bubba did struggle at times with Spanish, getting behind on assignments and not finding time to study enough. We had a few sessions at home where we went over telling time (that is a bit different in Spanish) and over the rules for conjugating verbs. For the most part, he was able to keep up with the assignments, perform adequately on quizzes and tests and maintain a C-average.

Fast forward to the end of the eleventh grade year; I received a phone call from his eleventh grade case manager regarding Bubba's schedule for twelfth grade. She went over her suggestions and I noticed that there was no foreign language in her list.

"What about Spanish?" I inquired.

"I think that might be too difficult for him," she replied. "He can take sociology as an elective. It will be easier."

"I was told last year by his case manager that it would be a good idea for Bubba to get two years of foreign language in high school. He said that many colleges expected that. Are you saying that is not correct?" I queried. Now I was in the mood to volunteer information.

I was trying to be as nice as possible, but the advice I had received over the years (other than the nice case manager that suggested a foreign language) was looking like a lot of inconsistent bologna! They said he would never be able to learn a foreign language and now Bubba was learning an adequate amount of Spanish with very little help.

"Sign him up for Spanish." No more argument. End of discussion.

Learning to Write

> *One of her teachers suggested that when Charlotte had to write a report or essay, I should get her to "free-write" first, to jot randomly everything that came into her head without thinking about punctuation, relevance, or "correctness" of any kind. Another strategy I learned from one of Charlotte's teachers, one that worked for Charlotte in the same way that free-writing does, was to get her to talk her ideas out first.*[42]

This chapter deals with learning to write, in the sense of organizing ideas and getting them written down, transcribed, dictated or typed. Hand-writing is the physical pen-to-paper activity. Proper grammar instruction, vocabulary, spelling and lots of reading all help the writer to write. For some reason, this organization process was also difficult for Bubba.

If you asked him to write a story about what he did over the weekend, he could easily recite back fact after fact, and in the proper order. One event might have been the most fun and then he would elaborate that event completely. That's all pretty good until the questions get harder.

---

[42] Dana Buchman and Charlotte Farber, *A Special Education, One Family's Journey Through the Maze of Learning Disabilities* (Da Capo Press, 2006).

In middle school and high school, students are expected to be able to write an opinion and to be able to craft a five-paragraph essay, or even a research paper. Bubba was struggling with just one paragraph.

One of the parents associated with an on-line support group claimed her little angel was declared by his teacher to be the best little writer in the class. She provided a basic format for a paragraph:

- Idea
- Example
- Fact/example
- Fact/example
- Restate

I presented this model for writing paragraphs to Bubba and he was willing to give it a try. This model provided the background for Bubba's paragraphs. With plenty of practice the paragraphs began as stiff, formula-followed writing, but with even more practice some transition words were interspersed. We had to itemize word options and substitutions so that all his paragraphs didn't sound exactly the same.

Along with the teaching at home, I enrolled Bubba in the reading and writing version of "The Program" that we were using for his math. The strengthening of his fundamentals with that program, along with the work in school, led to better writing and was evidenced in his two to five grade level jumps he experienced while he was enrolled in "The Program."

Preparing for his graduation test was another undertaking. There are extended response questions that required the student to respond reflective of his or her grade level, using proper grammar, spelling and paragraph structure.

For practice I had Bubba respond to practice questions by organizing his ideas into pros and cons. I would have him verbalize his answer first and prompt him to focus on answering the question that was asked. He developed two or three pros and likewise, two or three cons. He was familiar with a tool called the graphic organizer that he used at school and sometimes used that tool as well.

The organization of the essay then followed this structure:

- Opinion paragraph
- Pros paragraph
- Cons paragraph
- Summary paragraph

We developed alternate words for the pros, such as "positives are ..." or "good points were ..." and alternatives for cons, such as "negatives are ..." or "downfalls were ..." for use in the different paragraphs. The summary was difficult for Bubba, in that he would write the main idea again, sometimes word-for-word. He worked on starting his summary with phrases like "Despite the negative examples, the positives ..." Passing the graduation test in the tenth grade turned out to be too challenging for him and he missed the cutoff for proficiency by six points (out of 400), but he was definitely improving. A year prior, he was not close to passing the pretest.

When Bubba retested in eleventh grade on the writing portion of the graduation test, he scored close to the accelerated level of proficiency, the same year he was completing "The Program" for reading and writing. The work had paid off because this was a state-mandated graduation requirement.

I feel strongly about data, both objective and subjective and will go into that discussion in more detail later. It was clear from the data collected that Bubba had begun his educational career at a level that was above average.

Note in the following chart that prior to sixth grade, all of his objective measurements put him above the 100-level line labeled as "Average," or above the expected score. As his special education progressed into middle school, his standard scores in writing regressed and his standard scores all dropped below the average.

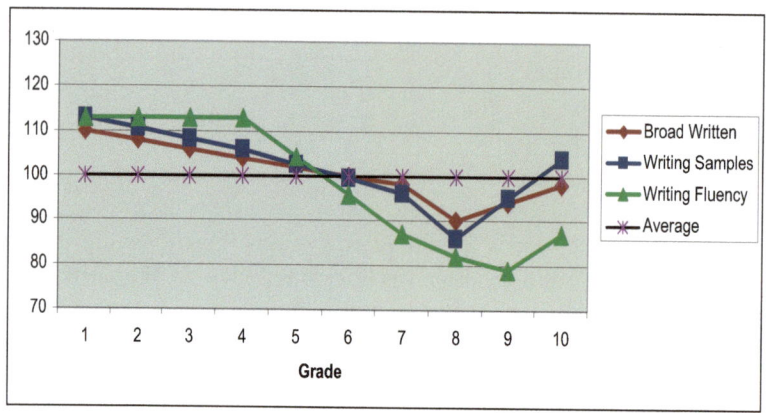

Tracking Writing Scores over Time

Unless something was done, there was no reason to believe that the regression would not continue. It is fairly clear, that by pressuring the school district for more attention, putting Bubba in "The Program," and providing additional help at home beginning in ninth grade, a major turnaround occurred. Note the V-shape of the writing components. This gave me encouragement that I had positively affected Bubba's writing skills and made appropriate choices in the approach. It paid off when he successfully passed his graduation test for writing, giving us both confidence and additional evidence that he was proficient.

Doodling

Participants who performed a shape-shading task, intended as an analogue of naturalistic doodling, concentrated better on a mock telephone message than participants who listened to the message with no concurrent task. This benefit was seen for monitoring performance and in scores on a surprise memory test. When monitoring performance was used as a covariate, the group effect became marginally significant, so it is not clear whether doodling led to better recall simply because doodlers noticed more of the target names or whether it aided memory directly by encouraging deeper processing of the material on the tape.[43]

At the beginning of the year in eleventh grade, we kicked off the IEP team meeting on a sunny, Tuesday morning. Bubba and I sat at the table along with District Coordinator 4, the high school coordinator, three teachers, an occupational therapist, the school psychologist and the high school guidance counselor. One of the teachers was his new case manager for eleventh grade. As usual we were completely outnumbered. Towards the end of the meeting, Bubba's new case manager and new homeroom teacher looked at Bubba and asked him to remove his chemistry binder from his book bag.

---

[43] Jackie Andrade, "What Does Doodling Do?" *Applied Cognitive Psychology*, 24 (1), 2009.

I was receiving the usual twenty or thirty emails a week from Bubba's case manager by this time regarding all sorts of issues. The volume was fairly predictable and I knew the email frequency would slow down by November or December. I wasn't sure what was up with the chemistry binder, but I was about to find out.

Bubba mumbled something and pulled the zipped-up, big blue binder from his book bag. He slid it part of the way across the large, square conference room table where it stopped. We all observed.

"Show everyone what you have been doing in chemistry class," the teacher demanded. Bubba pointed at the doodles that covered the exterior of the binder. I noticed song lyrics, famous hard rock band names, and strange shapes inked all over the front and back cover of the binder. He had done a lot of damage in a few short weeks.

"Instead of listening in class, Bubba is spending his time covering his binder with doodles!" the teacher complained.

"Is he bothering anyone?" I asked. I already had a suspicion what was going on.

"Yes, he is bothering the other students that are sitting near him," the teacher replied. Uh, right.

I looked at Bubba's English teacher and asked, "Does he do it in your class?" This was the same English teacher that Bubba had the year before so she was partially broken in.

The English teacher thought about that question for a moment and then commented, "No, he doesn't."

"How about in Spanish class?" I enquired.

"No, I don't think he does it in Spanish either," she responded.

The new and improved case manager sported a confused look and added, "He doesn't do it in math or history either."

"So he only does it in chemistry class?" I asked.

"Yes." The case manager was getting even more confused now, but I was getting a pretty clear picture of what was going on.

"I'm listening in class," Bubba spoke up.

"He's listening," I followed. "Is he only doing it when there are diagrams being presented?"

Now the case manager had a light flash on, I could tell. "Yes, he is only doing it when we are discussing diagrams!" She actually was getting excited.

"Bubba gets confused by diagrams," I explained. I had been over this topic with each team for the last four years. "While for most people diagrams help them understand a process, looking at diagrams confuses him. He is looking away on purpose to avoid confusion and is listening to try to understand."

You could have heard a pin drop in the room. Since the beginning of the school year, Bubba's teacher had been hounding him to pay attention during chemistry, when he had been paying attention the best way he knew how, by listening. For several weeks he had been berated about doodling and in thirty seconds I understood exactly what was going on. Yet I still was considered the least knowledgeable member of the team, the one with the memory.

Math Reasoning

> *That mathematics is a powerful, indeed indispensable, intellectual tool for the scientist does not mean that mathematics is science; it is the language, not the essence of science.*[44]

As Bubba finished the tenth grade, it was time to reflect on his status. He had gone from a partial resource room placement to general education with an aide, to general education for all his classes with no aide. Also, in tenth grade I began pulling back with the home support to see what would happen. He pulled a C average at a tough high school taking geometry, physics, English, world history and web design. He passed one of his high school graduation tests (reading) that had to be completed by twelfth grade, followed by history and writing when he retested.

His scores were headed up, as measured on the *Woodcock-Johnson Tests of Achievement*.[45] This test series measures student reading, writing and

---

[44] Lloyd Motz and Jefferson Hane Weaver, *The Story of Mathematics* (Avon Books, 1993).

[45] Richard W. Woodcock, Kevin S. McGrew and Nancy Mather, *Woodcock-Johnson® Tests of Achievement*, First edition published in 1977. Author is using *Woodcock-Johnson* from this point forward.

math competency and speed (fluency). In the three years since we began supplementing his education with "The Program," he had jumped five grade levels in math calculations and fluency, seven grade levels in writing samples, six grade levels in his broad reading, including his reading comprehension skills. These were all areas previously below grade level that now were at or above grade level. Similar results were obtained on the *WIAT*[46] tests (a battery of tests similar to the *Woodcock-Johnson*) performed by NeuroPsych.

There was one area that remained a little stubborn – math reasoning. Word problems. Math applications. He had jumped two and one half grade levels in the three years since seventh grade, which was close to the gains he had made in the prior seven grades, so his rate of acquisition had improved, but was still slightly less than a grade level per year, and still several levels below grade.

It was difficult to get good input from anyone on how to approach this problem. Some math theorists believe that math applications improve along with the improvement of the basic math skills. I asked his case manager at the school how a tenth grader could do tenth grade math applications when he was so far below grade, and how could we move him from grade level six, to seven, to eight? I received a shrug.

I asked the school's independent consultant who was the "expert" on kids like Bubba, if there were any direct instruction methods for word problems, or how she would suggest we approach it. My email and phone calls to her about the issue went unanswered. I even called her supervisor who returned my call and assured me I would get an answer. I am glad I didn't hold my breath.

Probably the most rational explanation of the issue came from the owner of the tutoring center where Bubba was attending for "The Program." She called it understanding the language of math. The school had spent years trying to teach Bubba to solve math word problems using pictures. I had noticed that his pictures had no resemblance to the math problem and explained this to his teachers, but they continued to use that method for six years, making absolutely no progress (not surprising given there was a visual-spatial, visual-organization deficit). Even after NeuroPsych

---

[46] David Wechsler, *Wechsler Individual Achievement Test*, The Psychological Corporation.

came to the school and explained the problem to the IEP team, they pressed onward with the same ineffective approach.

The tutor center owner had called it the language of math. I remember I was having a similar conversation with my PhD advisor one day and he stated that there should be no reason that a child could not learn math reasoning because it was really just translating English (or whatever language of choice) into algebra.

Given that the tutoring method used at the center had been effective for all the other stubborn areas, it seemed that applying this method to the problem of math reasoning would provide the best chances for improvement. That means:

- Start in the comfort zone with problems that are easy.
- Spend a short amount of time on problems every day or almost every day.
- Increase the difficulty in small increments.
- Provide repetition of each level of difficulty until there is mastery.

I obtained a few resources, including word problem books for grade six and above, and found a couple of math web sites that had interactive, language-focused math problems. We started the summer after tenth grade setting aside about ten minutes per day to work a problem from the word problem book I purchased. After completing about five or six days of work, the next session consisted of reviewing the previous problems.

On the first pass of a daily word problem, I would have Bubba completely read the problem, usually a paragraph. He would make a guess at what the solution method was. It was usually off track, but I did see improvement with repetition and practice. I would have him re-read the problem to see if there was any change in his approach. Early on in our sessions, there wasn't.

Then I would have him imagine he was involved in the circumstances of the problem. For example, one problem was about a pet shop owner who needed to feed his eight bunny rabbits. He had two cups of pellets. The problem wanted to know how much he could give to each rabbit. Because of the usage of the word "each," Bubba immediately interpreted the problem as a multiplication problem. I asked him to "be the owner" with the two cups of pellets.

"What do you have to do with the pellets?" I asked.

"Split them between the rabbits," he answered.

"And split means?"

"Divide," he said. Step-by-step is the way.

I had Bubba write the method he used to solve each problem in the space next to the problem in the book. Usually he didn't write the answer, because I didn't want to focus on what the answer was, but how to convert the words into a function, or algebraic equation. When we went back to review each problem, he would read the problem and then see the process he used to solve it. By this time his equation solving was very good; he just needed to learn how to set up the equation from the words provided.

As time went on, by eleventh grade Bubba had learned (after a couple of hundred problems) that when he read the problem the second time he thought about it differently. I continued to work with him on reading the problem a second time before he jumped to any conclusions about what was being said in the problem.

We continued doing daily word problems through the eleventh grade and on through the summer after eleventh grade, right into twelfth grade. There had been slow movement in the objective data related to math reasoning for several years and I was getting concerned that maybe this wasn't the proper approach or that the weakness in math reasoning could just not be improved.

When I attended the IEP meeting in the beginning of twelfth grade, I was given the results from his *Key Math* testing.[47] The test results contain separate scores for algebra, addition and subtraction, multiplication and division, foundations of problem solving and applied problem solving. I was most interested in the latter two, because they were the scores related to math reasoning and the weakness I was hoping we could improve.

The results are shown in the following graph that compares his scores from the beginning of eleventh grade to the beginning of twelfth grade.

---

[47] Copyright NCS Pearson, Inc.

To interpret these scores, a score between 90 and 110 may be considered average. When a score falls below 70, it is considered well-below average and when it lands above 130, it is well-above average. It also should be noted that a positive change from one year to the next implies a gain of more than one grade level for the year. If a student has a flat standard score from one year to the next, he is essentially holding his own or gaining the expected one grade level per year.

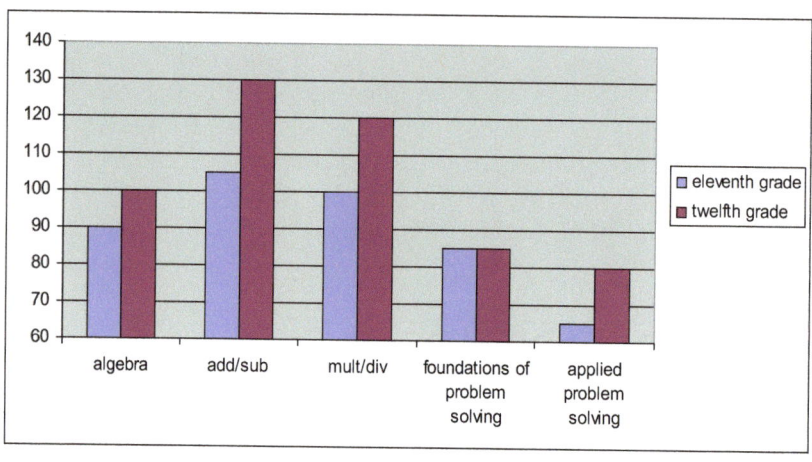

Comparison of Math Scores for Eleventh and Twelfth Grade

Considering that Bubba was still completing "The Program" for math each day, I was not surprised to see his basic addition, subtraction, multiplication and division skills continue to improve. He was firmly entrenched in the algebra levels of "The Program," and his algebra improved as well to solidly normal.

The foundations of problem solving remained in the low average, and there was still no gain or loss in the standard score, so he had essentially gained a year's worth of skill in a year. This was an improvement because in this greatest area of weakness, Bubba generally gained about ½ a year in a year. What was really encouraging was that there was a marked improvement in applied problem solving, from well-below average to below average (moving closer to average).

Maybe it was just a matter of plodding along in a repetitive consistent manner and focusing on those skills, but it did appear that the strategy was working. Like every other problem area, one-on-one tutoring with a direct instruction approach seemed to be the key and it took about five to ten minutes per day. My hope was that this improvement would carry over into improvements on his math and science graduation test requirements, and globally into better problem solving and interpretation skills.

Teacher Meetings – Part 2

> *"I have noticed an improvement in Bubba's maturity and willingness to take responsibility for his work independently over the course of the year. He is taking ownership for his assignments and does a nice job of getting involved and actively participating in each of his classes."*[48]

The eleventh grade teacher meeting was one of my more memorable meetings. I had driven to the school leaving plenty of time to park, walk to the building, and find the appropriate classrooms. By eleventh grade, the teachers met one-on-one for fifteen minutes per subject, probably because the attendance by many parents had slacked off by this point. Unfortunately, I was there on the wrong day and had to return two days later for my properly scheduled time. No problem.

I was scheduled to meet with the Spanish teacher, the math teacher, and the chemistry teacher. The comments were the usual and the mandatory grade sheets were handed over. One of the most interesting comments came from the math teacher. She was about 25 years old, blond and very professional. She explained how she ran her class and allowed the students to use notes if they needed them on the tests, and why she ran

---

[48] From Bubba's tenth grade case manager with a refreshing comment.

her class that way. She commented that Bubba was a hard worker and tried to get his homework done in class each day.

Then she said, "I think Bubba has a natural aptitude for math."

Hmm. I thought. This is interesting.

"He was still counting on his fingers at the end of seventh grade," I told her. She looked perplexed and gave me that "look" that I have seen when I told the ninth grade math teacher the same thing. His response was something like, "I don't believe that is true." I have Bubba counting on his fingers on video tape, however.

"He has been doing 'The Program' in math for the last three and a half years," I explained. "For a half an hour each day, seven days a week, 52 weeks a year he has been working at it."

"Well, it really works!" She said excitedly.

"Yes it does," I commented. I couldn't have had a better meeting, really, because it was just amazing to me that in four years he had evolved from unable to perform math to having a "natural aptitude."

State Mandated Graduation Tests and the Waiver

Waiver: The intentional relinquishment of a right, claim, or privilege.[49]

There are constant debates about "high stakes testing" and the impact on teaching methodologies. Opinions seem to vary about whether there is too much testing or not enough testing and whether there is too much "teaching to the test." I won't enter the debate. At Bubba's school, passing five state mandated graduation tests are an integral part of obtaining a regular diploma. These tests cover reading, writing, math, social studies and science.

It was our (Ex and my) opinion that Bubba should pass his state mandated graduation tests and complete four years of math, English, science and social studies. I had been warned years before by NeuroPsych to make sure that Bubba received a regular diploma and not an alternate diploma. An alternate diploma can be a certificate of completion or a special education diploma awarded for meeting IEP goals, but not necessarily state-mandated goals. NeuroPsych mentioned that some colleges do not consider an alternate diploma the same as a regular high school diploma.

---

[49] "Waiver" *The American Heritage Dictionary, Second College Edition* (Boston: Houghton Mifflin Company, 1976).

We clearly stated in the parent's section for IEP goals that we wanted Bubba to pass the reading, writing and math graduation tests, because in our minds that indicated that he was proficient according to State standards – the same standards applied to all students. Regardless of the nature of his challenges, we felt that it was the purpose of special education to attempt to remediate his "disabilities" to ensure he was proficient.

I began getting nervous in the tenth grade when the first set of results arrived and Bubba had only passed the reading portion of the test. When he retook the failed sections, he passed the social studies and writing portions. This was a major success because writing and math were his identified disabilities according to his IEP and he had performed at close to the "accelerated" level in writing. Unfortunately, he still had not passed the math and science portions as he proceeded through eleventh grade.

At the IEP meeting in eleventh grade, I brought up the subject of the state mandated graduation tests. "Bubba hasn't passed his math or science tests," I noted. "I would like to see him pass them both." Indeed, I did not believe he should graduate until he was deemed proficient.

"Don't worry about that," his case manager replied. "Those tests aren't that important and we can work around it." My red-flag sensors started going off because I heard the ambiguity in the statement and understood that the district personnel on the team didn't have much confidence in Bubba's ability to pass the tests. Nor did it sound like they would put much emphasis on achieving that goal, even though it clearly was important to Ex and me.

Bubba was able to retake the science and math portions of the test later in the year, and while he was close to passing both, the results again returned that he was not proficient. He had taken the regular algebra and geometry classes and received C level grades. He was enrolled in algebra II during the eleventh grade and was averaging about 80% in the class.

On "The Program" he was finishing the second to the last level of their high school curriculum and the math was starting to become easier, in that "The Program" topics were aligning with the concepts being covered in his algebra II class. He had worked hard for four years in the math portion of "The Program" by this time, continuously gaining ground and mastering the lower level concepts. He was finally at a point where he had caught up.

In the spring of eleventh grade, it was time for scheduling courses for the twelfth grade. One requirement for graduation at his school was the completion of a senior project. We were planning to have Bubba work on his senior project over the summer to get a head start and this involved him attending two weeks of video game development classes. As I was preparing to schedule the video gaming classes and his twelfth grade classes, I had another discussion with his case manager in April.

During the telephone call, she commented, "I am looking at Bubba's schedule and his transcripts here, and I'm thinking he should have the Brit Lit, and government, of course. He should take the geography – that would be four credits in science."

"That sounds good." I commented.

"I think a good class for him would be sociology and with senior seminar; that will be a lot of courses for him to take," she added casually.

"What about math?" I asked. "What about Spanish?" She wanted to get the Spanish dropped and I brought up the comments from his previous case manager that were all arguments for continuing the Spanish.

"I just thought with the senior project and all; it is very time consuming and a lot of work the entire senior year," she backpedaled.

"What about math," I asked again. "Shouldn't he get four years of math? And what about physical education?" I was really pushing it now. Bubba and I had determined years earlier that physical education during the school day broke his day up and allowed him a release for his frustrations.

Not taking math his senior year would also only give him three math credits when I knew taking four years of math is better for kids who may want to go on to college. And if a child is not proficient yet, shouldn't he continue taking classes to address the issue? He was already doing college algebra in "The Program" and doing well.

"When are the science and math proficiency test retakes scheduled for this summer?" I asked. "I want to avoid a conflict with the scheduling of his video game seminars."

"I wouldn't worry about the retakes," she stated. "The senior project is more important." She wanted to talk about his schedule for senior year. "I don't think he should take a math class. He will be busy with completing his senior project and will need the extra time."

"He hasn't passed his math graduation test yet. Don't you think he should continue taking math?" I failed to follow this logic.

"Well, okay. We do have a math class that I think would be good for him. We are using a computer program for instruction. The kids learn using the on-line system," the case manager informed me.

"What are they learning," I enquired.

"It is statistics, numbers." I started developing heartburn immediately. Years earlier, the IEP team had tried an on-line, computer-based math tutoring program for Bubba and they were never able to make it work for him. It was a total waste of time and a total failure. The instructor had thrown in the towel on that program after a month or so. I wanted no part of Bubba enrolled in another computer-based math course because I was finished with putting him in "waste-of-time" programs. I also could not understand how teaching statistics to a student before they understood calculus made sense.

"What other options are there?"

"Well, there is pre-calculus, but he doesn't have the grades for that. Or there is college algebra, but he wouldn't be able to get assistance in that class and he would have to do it on his own." The case manager was beginning to get annoyed with me, like so many before her.

I wanted to understand what would be covered in the college algebra class, and the case manager explained that they would be doing quadratic equations, factoring, and solving linear equations. I had been watching and helping him do these activities successfully at home already, so that class sounded like a natural to me. He could use the additional reinforcement of the concepts.

"Put him in the college algebra," I stated.

"Uh. Well." The case manager was hesitating for some reason. I truly didn't understand why. "I don't think that is a good idea. The other class would be on the computer and much better suited to Bubba."

I came to the conclusion that we were more interested in him passing the test than they were and that this was probably a common occurrence with the special education students. For kids with disabilities, passing these tests in math and science would require hard work and it just didn't appear to be a high priority for the school system.

"I think the college algebra will be just fine," I said, wanting to put the matter to bed and go back to work.

"Well, if you want him in that class, you're going to have to sign a waiver," she stammered. "You will have to sign a waiver."

Think about this. To this day, I really don't understand what the purpose of that statement was and whether such a device or form even exists. Because what would a waiver be? A form, signed by the parent that they have been advised by a teacher not to enroll their child in a class? Do it at your own risk? A form that does what? Relieves the school district of the responsibility of teaching the child? What does such a form say?

I told her sure, I would sign a waiver but oddly enough I never found out what a waiver was or even what it looked like. I scheduled him for the math retake that summer and two weeks of video game development training for his senior project.

When I relayed the information about the phone call to Ex, his first comment was, "Why would the school not continue working on math if he hasn't passed his proficiency yet?"

At the end of August, we were wrapping up the summer before Bubba's senior year. I had made a special weekend trip to Michigan to see my aunt turn 91 years old and was celebrating with her friends and my cousins. When I returned home, I pulled the accumulated mail out of the mailbox and saw that the results from the math graduation test retake were in the mail. I ripped open the envelope and scanned though the material to see "PASSED." Bubba was "PROFICIENT" in math. I let

Ex know immediately and there was a great yell heard for miles! Ex began shouting, "Take that, so-and-so," referring the myriad of disbelievers and naysayers we had encountered along the way.

September brought the final (at least I hoped it was) IEP meeting during Bubba's twelfth grade year. The case manager (another new one) wanted to continue focusing on Bubba's writing. She emailed me her thoughts on Bubba's IEP and had provided several possible IEP goals, most of which were related to Bubba's writing organization.

"I see Bubba has passed all his graduation tests except science. We can waive the requirement to pass the science proficiency," she emailed me. "It causes too much stress."

Too much stress for whom? I emailed her back that I did not want Bubba waived from the requirement to pass the science proficiency. I had purchased his class ring, was having his senior portraits scheduled and ordering his graduation cap and gown, but I had made up my mind that if he didn't pass, then he could just come back for another year. I didn't think Bubba seemed all that stressed about taking the test.

At the IEP meeting, I reiterated my message that if Bubba did not pass his science proficiency, he would not graduate. I was not going to sign anything to waive that requirement. We dropped most of the additional writing goals and added additional tutoring twice a week for science concepts and measurements. (Bubba sometimes still did not apply the basic measurements and conversions consistently.)

And when we had the IEP meeting his senior year, I waited for the waiver to be added to the stack of paperwork, but it never appeared. What happened to that line of bunk? The waiver never appeared because the system has no memory. Not one person on the IEP team (except me) knew anything about the school district requiring a waiver for Bubba to take college algebra his senior year. And I didn't bring it up either!

Bubba took the science proficiency in October and in early January he sent me an email at work that he had some "EXTREMELY good news." Indeed, he had passed his science proficiency and followed that up with a successful completion of his senior project in January as well.

There are large percentages of "regular" education children that do not pass their State mandated proficiencies, and a much larger portion of special education students that do not pass. I am confident that Bubba would not have passed his proficiencies if Ex and I had not made that a consistent expectation of the school system. I am also sure that by passing the proficiencies, Bubba's confidence and self-esteem increased. Sure, we could have focused more on writing his senior year, but he had already scored in a high proficiency range on that test. We wanted him to demonstrate the required proficiency level in reading, writing, math, and in all five areas if it was possible.

And Bubba proved it was possible.

Statistical Note on the Passage of State Mandated Proficiencies

Below are some sample statistics from the states of Ohio and Washington. Most states post their proficiency rates online, listing special needs students as disabled.

State of Ohio: Graduation rates and proficiency rates – The graduation rate for disabled students in Ohio was 73% in 1996 and rose to 85% in 2006. The graduation rate for non-disabled students in Ohio was 80% in 1996 and rose to 87% in 2006.

The proficiency rates are much lower for disabled students. For example, in 2006 the percentage of general education students not passing the graduation test by 11th grade was 6%; the rate for students with a disability was 44%. The rate of general education students not proficient in reading was 3% while for those with a disability, the rate of non-proficiency was 35%. Remember, 85% of the students with a disability graduate. (Apparently many of them are not proficient in math and reading.)

State of Washington - Washington was identified as highly rated by the U.S. Department of Education, meeting expectations for all their measurement indicators. In 2007, there were 124,000 students in special education in 295 districts. The graduation rate of students with IEPs getting a regular diploma compared to the graduation rate of all students getting a regular diploma was 68%, and 55% received them on-time.

The special education enrollment rate in Washington is around 12% of the students. The percentage of tenth grade students with IEPs that were proficient in reading was 37% compared to 85% for students without IEPs. The percentage of tenth grade students with IEPs that were proficient in math was 9% compared to 54% for those without IEPs.

After sifting through federal data and data from several states, the story was the same (I looked at Minnesota and California and got the same story). There are students not in special education that are graduating without being proficient in math and reading. The percentage of students in special education graduating without being proficient in math and reading is much higher and there is a much larger percentage of students in special education today than there were twenty, or even ten years ago. And unfortunately, they are not remediated because once they enter special education, they rarely leave.[50]

---

[50] National Center for Education Statistics, "The Condition of Education 2009," See www.nces.ed.gov/programs/coe for annual reports.

"The Guy Down Below"

Part 3 – Motivating School Administrators

While providing the interventions with private tutoring, vision therapy, typing, math instruction, writing instruction, cursive instruction and other home activities, I began to feel that Bubba's special education was occurring primarily outside of the school day. I was angry and felt that the school district should at least reimburse me for the tutoring as it had been recommended by the professionals; the district had agreed to provide it, but had neglected to follow through.

In addition to attending meetings and providing interventions, in tandem and in frustration, I began building charts based on factual data, reading hundreds of special education cases, and getting strategically more aggressive in my dealings with the school administration.

Data, Bad Data and Useless Data

> *An initial hypothesis leads by a process of deduction to certain necessary consequences that may be compared with data. When consequences and data fail to agree, the discrepancy can lead, by a process called induction, to modification of the hypothesis. A second cycle in the iteration is thus initiated. The consequences of the modified hypothesis are worked out and again compared with data (old or newly acquired) that in turn can lead to further modification and gain of knowledge.*[51]

Most of my working life has been spent fiddling around with data. Data architecture, data modeling, data mining, querying data, reporting on data, manipulating data, statistically analyzing data and cleansing data. Many times, while reporting or analyzing data, bad data emerges, requiring cleansing. I've seen some organizations skip the cleansing step and instead ignore the bad data or employ several people in an effort to work around bad data.

Reports tend to be used by managers and decision makers so they can adjust business operations and understand the impact of these

---

[51] George E.P. Box, William G. Hunter, and J. Stuart Hunter, *Statistics for Experimenters, An Introduction to Design, Data Analysis, and Model Building* (New York: John Wiley and Sons, 1978).

adjustments. For example, an organization might offer a promotion on an item and analyze sales figures before and after the promotion, or compare the promotion to another promotion in an attempt to determine if one promotion provides a greater benefit than the other. Information technology folks use data to understand if one technology or methodology provides better system performance than another to provide justification for purchases, enhancements, personnel and even computer code changes.

It is fairly common sense to see and show that even under simplified conditions, there is a detrimental impact by having bad data used to make decisions. With all these instances of bad data around and all these folks wanting to make good decisions, it was relatively easy to stay gainfully employed, fighting the good fight against bad data.

The summer before Bubba entered eighth grade, I had requested a mediation as there had been such a downward trend (I believed) in his reading, writing and math. The lack of any real change in his programming after the informative visit by NeuroPsych left me stunned. And the continued denial of common sense requests by District Coordinator 2 and Bubba's IEP team culminated to the point where I was motivated to get more aggressive. That was when I called the State Special Education office and pleaded my case. The representative there encouraged me to request mediation and he actually put together the bulk of the arrangements for me.

As I drafted the mediation request, I tried to put together objective data points to back up my position. Fortunately Bubba had been seen in the first, fourth and seventh grades by either a psychologist or neuropsychologist, each of whom performed the same test series – the *Woodcock-Johnson* test. That was the bulk of objective data available. School grades were all As and Bs for the most part, but he was still counting on his fingers at that time. He had only passed the reading proficiency in seventh and eighth grade, but in courses like math, science and history he was not proficient. And his *Woodcock-Johnson* test scores showed that he was several levels below grade.

I looked for other data and found a reading score on a *STAR* test. This is the *Standardized Testing and Reporting* used by many states to do student testing. I also found math computation and word problem scores from the *Brigance*[52] test, a different test used by many districts to test reading, writing and math. The *Woodcock-Johnson* test showed a downward trend in his reading, writing and math standard scores; where over time he had regressed from at or above average, to well below average in all three. It was impossible for me to understand how the school managed data regarding Bubba and his performance at school. If I didn't have the *Woodcock-Johnson* test scores from each of the three years, I would have had practically nothing, and indeed no objective data comparing year over year progress.

The mediation was scheduled just prior to the beginning of Bubba's eighth grade year and was held at the middle school. I prepared my list of requests prior to the session and convinced my mother and Ex to attend the session with me.

The mediation was held in a large conference room that could comfortably seat about 20 people. The three of us entered the room (Ex, Mom and I), sat down and were surrounded by ten or twelve school representatives. Was it meant to be intimidating? We were definitely outnumbered.

One of my first requests was specific to collecting more objective data regarding Bubba's reading, writing and math performance. I requested that Bubba be tested on the *Woodcock-Johnson* test in eighth grade so we could see how much progress was made in eighth grade. We could compare those results to the same test performed in first, fourth and seventh grade.

"He just had that test last year," District Coordinator 3 volunteered. We found out during the introductions that District Coordinator 2 had retired over the summer. Now I had a new face to deal with. "He can only have that test one time per year."

"Do it at the end of the year," I suggested. "I would like to see him advance a grade level this year in math and writing as measured by the *Woodcock-Johnson* testing and have that as a goal."

"You don't want to do that," she argued. "There's no way to measure during the year what the progress toward the goal is because the test can

---

[52] Copyright Curriculum Associates, LLC.

only be performed once per year." I had heard that the first time, but I thought measuring once per year was an improvement over the current three year interval plan. (Also I found out later that there was a "B" version of the test that could be performed allowing measurement twice per year.)

"I want him measured on the *Woodcock-Johnson* test at the end of the school year," I insisted. "Then I will know what grade level he is at and can compare it to seventh grade."

The school psychologist chimed in next. She explained that the grade level wasn't really a grade level because it measures the student against a broad national average. "Not only that, but as he progresses, so do all the other students, so it really isn't that useful. I don't know why parents are so interested in grade level anyway."

"We can use the *Brigance* test," District Coordinator 3 said.

"I don't understand," I said. "The *Brigance* test says he is at 2.0 on word problems. Does that mean he is at only a second grade level?"

"No," the special education teacher explained. "You can't translate the number to a grade level equivalent. It has to do with the level of skills he has mastered."

"What grade level is he then?" I asked.

"You can't go by that," she responded. I was getting a feeling I was in a maze. District Coordinator 3 solved the problem with this one. "Let's use the *Brigance* measurement in the goal because we can run that test more than one time per year and measure progress during the year." Lots of heads nodded.

This would have been useless data to me. Why? Suppose he went from a level 2.0 to a level 3.0. This is great progress, right? Except an increase of 1.0 level might translate to learning the equivalent of one-tenth of a grade, or one-tenth of what the typical student learns. Or it might translate to five times what the typical student learns. There was no way to tell or they weren't able to explain it to me. And if the child learns, for example, at a rate of one-half the typical population without special education, we would expect to see the child learn at a faster rate with special education, right? But with useless data, there is no way to tell.

And given the data that was available there was no way to tell what Bubba's current rate of knowledge acquisition was, except for the scores from the *Woodcock-Johnson* test.

"I want him tested again on the *Woodcock-Johnson* test at the end of the year," I insisted. I think they finally caught on that I was not budging in my position. The *Woodcock-Johnson* test and the *Brigance* testing were added to his IEP which ended up being a good thing, because they remembered to test him at the end of the year on the *Woodcock-Johnson* test, but somehow forgot about measuring him during the year with the *Brigance*.

We insisted that Bubba required one-on-one tutoring and finally got agreement from the school district during the mediation that math and writing tutoring were needed. I wanted to continue him on "The Program" because, after two months, he already had progressed to mental math instead of using his fingers. The district wanted to use a computer-based tutoring program.

"Have you used it before?" I asked. Heads turned and eyes shifted.

"No," District Coordinator 3 responded.

"Then do you have any information about how effective it is with kids like Bubba?"

"They have a web-site you can look at." This time the middle school vice principal chimed in. It was not clear to me why this man was even in attendance at the meeting. Our only experience with him and his only experience with Bubba was the horrific way he handled the bullying/band situation. They were offering a web-site to look at, or in other words, they really had no data on the program's effectiveness.

"Please, give it a chance," District Coordinator 3 pleaded.

Here's an example where I had a little observational data related to Bubba's progress using "The Program," as opposed to no data regarding the program the school district was advocating. And I had a gut feeling to boot. But I caved. (I don't think that would ever happen again, but who knows – the caving part.) I agreed to let them use my son as a guinea pig on their untried and untested computer-based math tutoring program with no data related to its effectiveness. I relented only because I had "The Program" in my back pocket.

We also agreed during the mediation that Bubba would get two hours of writing tutoring each week. This progress was to be measured using some internally created rubric that I still don't understand. I was not too concerned about measurement using the mysterious rubric because writing was also going to be measured on the *Woodcock-Johnson* test.

So after two days of mediation, the district came to agreement with Ex and me on the issues that I wanted most. Bubba was to get math and writing tutoring and he was to get measured at the end of the year. Ex, Mom and I left the sessions in amazement at some of the comments and a little skeptical, but we were hopeful that progress was in the making.

Unfortunately, two months into the computer-based math tutoring, it had become clear to the middle school special education coordinator (she was to become District Coordinator 4) that the program was not working. Fortunately, we never took him out of "The Program" we had already enrolled him in, the program that my gut told me was working.

"We would like to discontinue the computer-based math program," future District Coordinator 4 let me know in a telephone call one day. "Is that okay with you?" she asked.

"How has his progress been?" I enquired.

"It's not working. He doesn't like it and it takes too long to get him set up and it's taking away from other school work," she said.

"Do you have any data related to his progress?" I asked.

"We can get data."

"I can't make a decision if there's no data so I don't know whether to tell you to leave him in or take him out," I said. No data. In order to get data from a computer-based system, I was pretty sure it was a matter of printing out a report. "Can you send me a copy of the report on his progress?"

"Sure," she replied.

She provided me with a report from the computer about three months later. Yes, it took three months to print out the report. I read the report and still could not figure out what progress had been made because it only listed when he had logged on and off the system. Bad data, or was it just useless data again? I could tell from the log-on dates that the district had made the decision to stop implementing the program shortly after our phone conversation, so it wasn't totally useless data, in the case where a parent would want to present a complaint! She had provided me useless data regarding Bubba's performance while at the same time providing documentation that the school district was violating the mediation agreement.

At the end of the year we met with the psychologist who had performed the *Woodcock-Johnson* testing. Math calculations were up four grade levels, math fluency was up three grade levels and word problems were up one and one-half grade levels. Better data. A fluke perhaps, but when measured again at the end of ninth grade (at the persistence of those danged parents), results were even higher after another year of tutoring on "The Program."

I became convinced that periodic, consistent, grade-level equivalent measurements were required, particularly in Bubba's case, where proficiency tests were not passed and objective data was lacking. I understood grade level equivalent and this worked well for backing up complaints against the school district as complaints became increasingly necessary. Without good objective data, there is "progress" as long as someone says so.

Making the Chart

> *Remember: All important educational decisions - from eligibility, the services in your child's IEP, how progress is measured - are based on test scores.*[53]

The mediation came about after numerous unresolved requests regarding concerns about Bubba's education. I had called the State Department of Education in frustration and I was referred to the Department of Special Education where I felt that I was heard. The representative who listened to my concerns was the man who suggested that I initiate the mediation session with the school district. He had asked me to document my concerns and send them to him and he would contact the school district to set up the meeting.

As I organized my thoughts, I tried to prioritize the issues that were important to me. "He's not making progress in reading, writing and math," I thought. There were other issues regarding having a buddy, social skills and occupational therapy as well. Bubba hated the resource room. I wanted my mediation request to be factual, so I began getting my facts together. This included delving through piles of papers that were stuffed in bureau drawers, bags of school papers in the basement,

---

[53] "Cold Hard Numbers and Successful IEP Meetings," Resources provided at www.wrightslaw.com.

old grade cards and progress reports. I went to the school as well and requested my son's records to insure that I wasn't missing any available data. It led me to conclude that it would be a lot more efficient if I had kept all the records in one place using some type of organization method.

Nevertheless, I perused through the data to put together charts of how well Bubba was doing. Fortunately, I had measurements from first, fourth and seventh grades that were fairly complete and they used the same testing methodology. What good would the data be if they were not completed using the same measurement method?

Making the charts brought up these two important issues – I had to make and maintain an organized and complete set of records, and I had to get measurements at regular intervals using the same measurement method. Not only was it important to use the data to make a chart so that I could concisely explain my concerns to someone else, it was key to determining the legitimacy of my concerns.

The making of charts and maintenance of them over time allowed me to track effectiveness of different interventions. This was implemented by measuring before the intervention and comparing to measurements after the intervention. The chart and accompanying data allowed me to see if a program was working as well as I felt it was working, and if (for example) moving Bubba out of the resource room was as beneficial to him academically as I felt it was.

The measurement method that I insisted upon each year was the *Woodcock-Johnson* tests. This wasn't because I was convinced it was the only or the best testing method, but because he had been measured in first, fourth and seventh grade using that test and I wanted his data to be collected using the same testing method. Otherwise, it gets confusing to try to relate a test score from one method to a test score from another method. It requires guesswork and interpolation and compromised any validity of understanding.

The *Woodcock-Johnson* tests are considered validated, have a break down of the components of reading, writing and math, and scores are produced for grade level equivalent, age equivalent and standard scores. I used the grade level equivalent and standard scores to help understand Bubba's progress.

Grade Level Equivalent Chart

The grade level equivalent chart by subject(s) (reading, writing, and/or math) uses the student's grade as the X-axis. In the chart shown below, the line "Average Score" shows the average peer grade level by grade. This is actually very simple because the expectation is that the average student will gain one grade level per year. In the first grade, the average student is at a first grade level and by grade four, the average student is at a fourth grade level. The line called "Student Score" represents a fictitious child being measured.

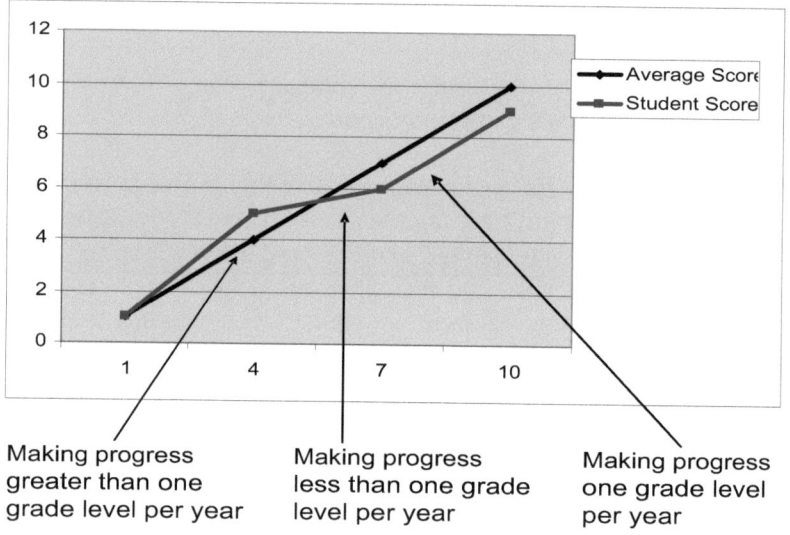

Sample Grade Level Chart

I have presented three scenarios in this chart to help explain how to interpret the grade level chart. In all three scenarios, the student is making progress. In this type of chart, lack of progress would be represented as a flat line, and deterioration of progress would have a negative or downward slope.

In the first scenario, from grade one through grade four, this student went from grade level one to grade level five. During that interval the student was making an average of more than one grade level gain per year. Thus, the "Student Score" line is above the "Average Score" line up through grade four.

In the second scenario, from grade four through grade seven, the student went from a grade level five to grade level six. The student is making some progress, but the rate of growth has slowed compared to the previous scenario, and by grade seven, the student is below grade level. The rate of growth in the first scenario is five grade levels in four years, or 1.25 grade level gains per year. The rate of growth in the second scenario is one grade level in three years or .33 grade level gains per year.

From grade eight through grade ten, the student went from a grade level six to grade level nine. The student is making progress at a rate of three grade levels in three years, or one grade level per year. This is the "average" rate, but at this point, because of the slower progress in the second scenario, the student remains one grade level behind his or her peers. The student score line is below the average grade level line from grade eight through ten.

Standard Scores Chart

The standard scores chart shows the data in a different way. Comparisons are made to the average by comparing to the value of 100. In standard scoring, 100 is the peer average on any particular measure, for example, reading comprehension, writing samples or math calculation.

In this chart, there are also three scenarios. From grade one through four, the standard score moves from 110 to 90. This means that over that time period, the student has gone from above average to below average. This would correspond to grade level scores where the student is making slow, no, or backward progress. It is a regression in the sense that compared to the student's peers; the student is losing ground or getting further behind his peers.

In the second scenario, in grade four through seven in this chart, the student's scores are a flat line. The standard score in fourth grade is the same as the score in seventh grade. A flat line on the standard score chart would correspond to grade level gains of one grade level per year. In this scenario, the student is making progress at the same rate as his or her peers. The student is not losing ground or gaining ground compared to his peers.

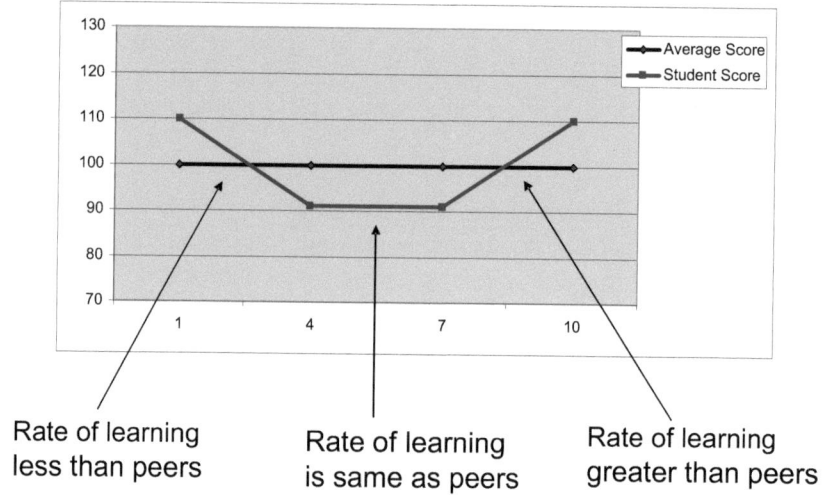

Sample Standard Score Chart

In the third scenario, in grade eight through grade ten of this chart, the student's standard scores move from 90 back up to 110. For this scenario, the student is gaining at a rate faster than his or her peers, and this would correspond to grade level gains of more than one grade per year.

Reading Progress Chart

To request the mediation in a concise manner, I began by creating Bubba's reading progress chart. This was the summer after Bubba's seventh grade year before the beginning of Bubba's eighth grade year, and I had scores for only grade one, four, and seven.

The chart shows the standard scores for three components of the broad reading; comprehension, fluency and letter word identification (spelling). Bubba was strongly above grade level (> 100) for all three components in the first grade. By fourth grade his scores for comprehension and fluency began to lag and actually fell below grade level by seventh grade.

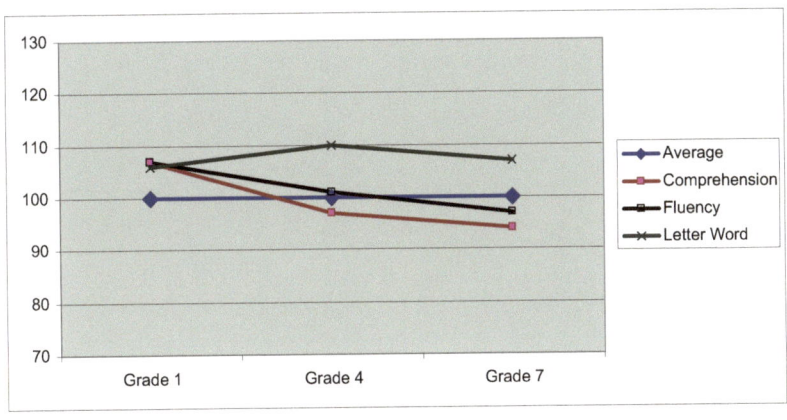

Reading Grade Levels for First, Fourth and Seventh Grade Using Standard Scores

It was in grade four that the district decided that Bubba should be in the resource room for reading. He was already in the resource room for writing and math. But moving Bubba to the resource room for more intense, personalized instruction didn't stop the lagging progress for Bubba. His standard scores continued to drop for all three components over the next three years. However his letter-word scores remained above grade level. This data did not support the premise that the resource room improved his reading skills. Note that a standard score of 95 is not a large deviation from "average," but nevertheless, the continued downward trend indicated he was not progressing at one grade level per year.

The grade level equivalents are shown in the next chart for Bubba's reading in grade one, four and seven. At first glance, the chart may look good because the lines are sloped upward. All three components are above grade level in grade one. By grade four, the comprehension had slipped below grade to a grade equivalent of around 3.5. And by the seventh grade, comprehension had only risen to a grade equivalent of 5.0, and Bubba was two grade levels behind! Reading fluency had also dropped below grade level while the letter word category remained strong (consistent with Bubba's exceptional spelling skills).

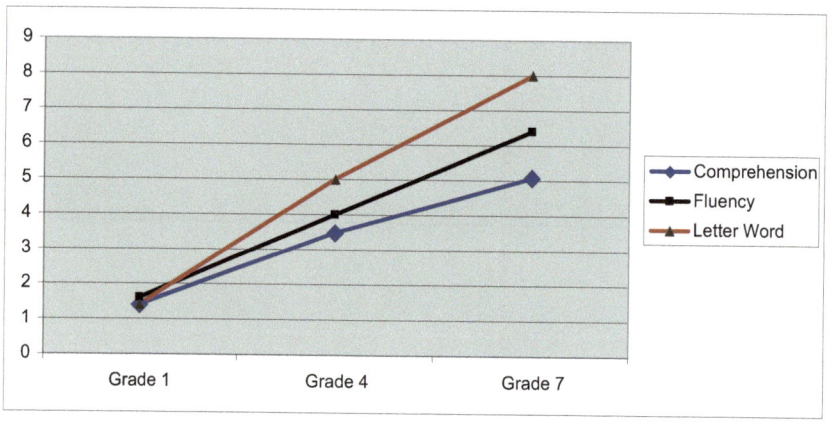

Reading Grade Levels for First, Fourth and Seventh Grade Using Grade Equivalent Scores

I went on to generate charts for math and writing in preparation for the mediation, and I became dismayed after creating them. Writing progress was non-existent, and math progress was around a half grade level per year. At those rates, with five years of schooling left, Bubba would graduate high school at a fifth grade level in writing, a sixth grade level in math and a seventh grade level in reading.

I presented my issues supported by facts to the State Department of Education. While I thought that Bubba was not making progress in reading and math, he was making progress. But the rate of his progress left him falling farther and farther behind. I used these charts to explain my position regarding the need for tutoring or one-on-one instruction, for Bubba to gain at a faster rate. I was sure that Bubba was not getting sufficient one-on-one instruction in the resource room.

Bubba was already out of the resource room for reading by the time the mediation was scheduled. It was clear by the data, expressed simply in the charts, that the placement in the resource room was minimally improving his reading and math skills, and having no effect on his writing skills.

Reading Progress In and Out of the Resource Room

I will jump forward a little to show with scores what happened over time with Bubba's reading. When he was removed from the general education class in the fourth grade his broad reading and reading comprehension scores were around the fourth grade level. From grade four to grade seven he was placed into the resource room for reading, a measure largely determined because of class scheduling difficulties and the promise of individualized instruction. This individualized instruction put Bubba further behind his peers.

At the end of seventh grade, after the long, drawn out and sometimes heated meeting with District Coordinator 2, the Assistant District Superintendent (long before she developed the "red neck" and while she was still a principal) and the special education teacher (the one who constantly looked at her fingernails), my mother, Ex and I argued about moving Bubba from the resource room back into the general education classroom. After three hours of discussion (I had figured out by this time that long meetings could be my friend), it was finally decided that he could move back into the general education classroom on a "trial" basis. When I told Bubba he was thrilled.

I continued tracking Bubba's reading scores, and in subsequent years asked for them to be completed each year. From fourth though seventh grade, while in the resource room, Bubba gained approximately two grade levels, or gained at a rate of 2/3 grade per year in his broad reading scores. After Bubba moved back into the general education class for literature in the eighth grade, and remained out of the resource room thereafter, the grade level gain in reading comprehension jumped to three or more grades per year.

Note that we added "The Program" for reading and writing in the beginning of ninth grade, which provided an extra boost. "The Program" that I added to his home-based special education was a direct instruction reading and writing program as suggested by NeuroPsych. I concluded there was no good argument for putting Bubba in the resource room for reading, particularly as it also affected his self-esteem.

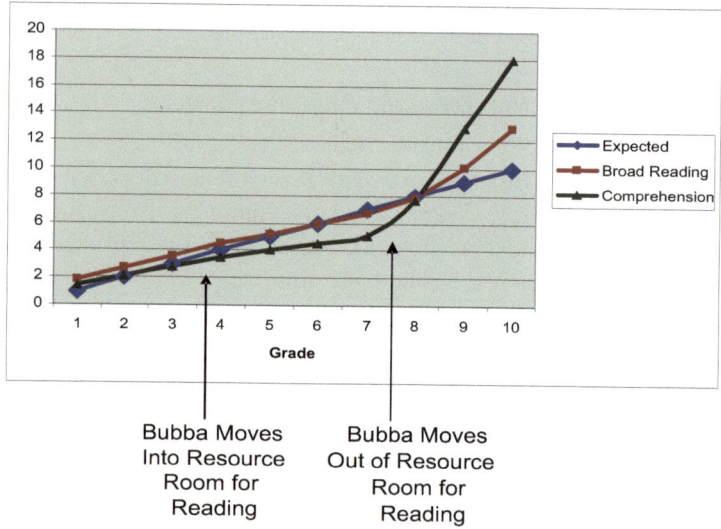

Bubba Moves Into Resource Room for Reading

Bubba Moves Out of Resource Room for Reading

Reading Scores In and Out of the Resource Room

The use of the chart only supported the decision to move Bubba out of the resource room. The chart provided objective data that supported Bubba's "feelings" about the resource room and my intuition about the resource room. Of course, one could argue that Bubba's grade level gains had nothing to do with the resource room or "The Program," and that maybe some other factor coincidentally was influencing his performance. But without the measurements, all conclusions would have been based on subjective data.

Objective Data

> *Measurement is direct when the student is observed performing the behavior of interest in the natural context or environment for that skill (or a permanent product from the performance is assessed). Measurement is objective when the frequency and/or quality of student performance is recorded in standard units of number and/or time (e.g., number of words read correctly per minute). Measurement is frequent when it occurs on a regular basis, ideally each time instruction occurs.*[54]

On one phone discussion with District Coordinator 3 shortly after I filed my first complaint with the State Department of Education, I was informed that one of Bubba's scores was average because it was 85, which was exactly between the range of 82 to 88. She explained that this was listed on the output of the *Woodcock-Johnson* test. She did not understand how to read the test scores and she was the district coordinator.

The average standard score on a *Woodcock-Johnson* subtest is 100. An average score of 100 is also the average on the *WIAT* testing and IQ testing because they are based off an assumption that the scores are

---

[54] William L. Heward, "Ten Faulty Notions About Teaching and Learning That Hinder the Effectiveness of Special Education," *The Journal of Special Education*, 36 (4), 2003.

"bell" shaped (or statistically have an underlying normal distribution), with 100 in the center of the "bell." Depending on the tester, they will indicate that around 90 to 110 is average.

What the coordinator had mistakenly explained to me was a confidence interval around Bubba's standard score, which means that the evaluator believed Bubba's score was an 85, but was highly confident that it was somewhere between 82 and 88. This is about two to three grade levels below average, by the way, not average. Given that some of his scores were in the low 80s at times, there were areas where he was approximately four levels below grade.

I sighed in frustration and I had to discontinue the conversation because there was no way I could educate this woman on standard scores, nor would it do any good to try because I am only a parent. Okay, I have a statistics degree and a doctorate in engineering but what does that mean? She was the professional.

In the next chart, the standard scores for broad reading, writing and math are shown for grades one, four and seven. The term "broad" is used because the score encapsulates a group of subtests in each of the relevant areas.

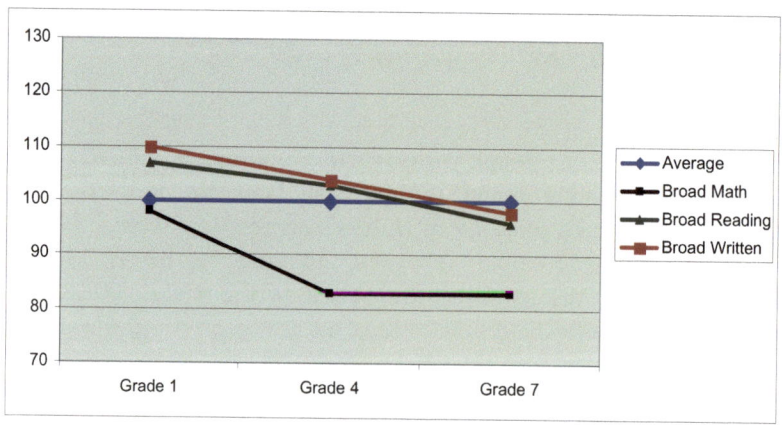

Standard Scores for Reading, Writing and Math for First, Fourth and Seventh Grade

The downward slope doesn't necessarily mean that Bubba wasn't making any progress, but as the "average" child moved from first to fourth to seventh grade, Bubba was gaining at a much lower rate. A flat line would indicate that he was gaining one grade level per year and a line with a positive slope would indicate that he was "closing the gap" on his peers.

The line marked average is at the 100 level. This divides the tested individual's scores into above and below average. Reading and writing were above average in first grade, with math about average. By seventh grade, all the subject areas were below average, and had regressed. This type of downward slope is called a regression in the student's standard scores.

The second chart shows the same broad reading, writing and math grade level equivalents for grades one, four and seven. Reading and math show progress while the writing starts to flatten out after fourth grade. The graph shows Bubba at a fourth grade level in math in seventh grade.

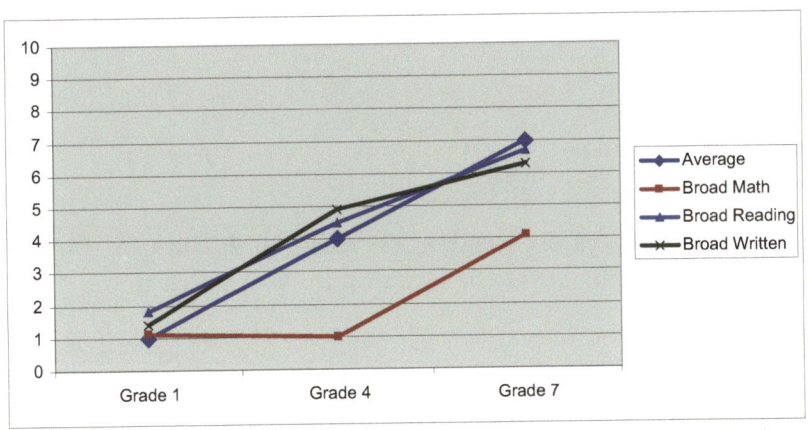

Grade Equivalents for Reading, Writing and Math for First, Fourth and Seventh Grade

Right after seventh grade, Ex and I began advocating much more actively, starting with a request for mediation to get tutoring for Bubba in writing and math. The data shown in the chart above helps explain why. We also kept him enrolled in "The Program" for math during the eighth grade and subsequently added the out of school reading and writing program for him in ninth grade. The district consistently did not provide the services they agreed upon in the mediation so this turned out to be a very wise decision.

In the next chart, the eighth and ninth grade scores are added, using the standard scores. The data supports the theory that the tutoring provided outside of school worked. Notice the V-shape of the math standard scores – a turn-around from getting further away from the "average" to moving closer and closer to the "average." Similarly, the writing scores have the V-shape subsequent to the addition of the writing tutoring we provided.

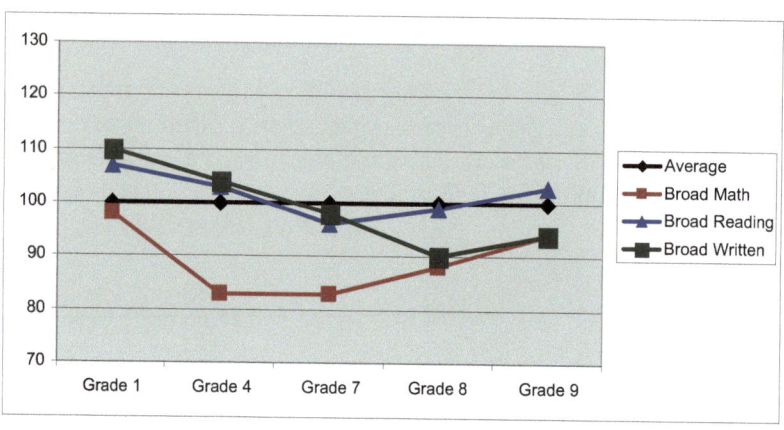

Standard Scores for Reading, Writing and Math for First, Fourth, Seventh, Eighth and Ninth Grade

The positive slopes in reading, writing and math all indicate a greater than one grade level gain per year, which all happened subsequent to moving Bubba out of the resource room and providing the tutoring. Reading moved back to above average by ninth grade. Math and writing moved to around the 95% range by ninth grade, which was much closer to average.

In the next chart, the grade level equivalents are shown for broad reading, writing and math with the addition of the years for eight and ninth grade. The first block shows the grade level gains for grades 1 through 7. The average yearly gains in reading, writing and math are all less than a grade level gain per year.

In the eighth grade, Bubba was moved out of the resource room for reading and we added math tutoring. Notice the high spike in the math grade level gain for eighth grade and again in ninth grade. Reading gains moved to one grade level gain per year in eighth grade, followed by a 1.5 grade level gain in ninth grade.

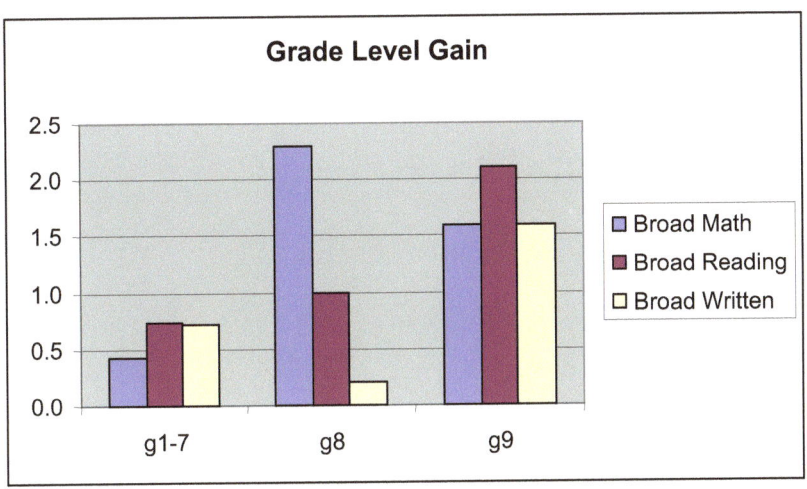

Grade Level Gain Rate for 1-7, 8th and 9th Grade

The third block, marked "g9" or ninth grade shows a dramatic improvement in writing as well, when we added the additional writing tutoring. All the subjects show 1.5 or higher grade level gains by the ninth grade. Instead of progress at about one-half grade level per year, after adding the tutoring, the gains are all dramatically improved.

I found it reassuring to have objective scores to track progress on an annual basis. Feedback from Bubba's teachers progressively got better and Bubba was definitely more confident. His skills sure seemed better and the data also showed good progress. The eighth grade evaluation was not a fluke as there were similar, even better gains evident in the ninth grade evaluation.

Subjective Data

> *Position of the School: Student made progress towards meeting his IEP goals in reading, writing and mathematics as well as in his inclusion science class. Position of the Neuropsychologist: In general, most of [Student's] basic academic skills lie in the Borderline range or below, with most skills lying between the second and fifth grade range (between four and seven years below his current grade placement).*[55]

It would be unwise to rely solely on objective data. Ideally, the subjective data and objective data would convey a consistent story. As much as I like numbers for expressing progress, there are problems with test results as they may only indicate how a student did in a snapshot of time, or on a particular day. And if the student didn't sleep well, or was just feeling surly, or if the test environment was distracting as opposed to quiet, the results can change. The test may have wording issues that cause the student to not understand the questions. Having objective results from multiple tests helps firm up the reliability of the numbers, and having subjective data provides even more confidence that results are, or are not being achieved. Having objective data and

---

[55] Commonwealth of Massachusetts, Special Education Appeals, BSEA #09-3554.

subjective data from multiple sources gives a parent a more reliable view than having only one set of test results, or only teacher input, or only a mother or father's gut instinct.

The problem with subjective data is that it is subjective. This means that two observers can view the same student and provide different, identical or conflicting feedback. So getting the subjective data over time from more than one observer helps mitigate the one-sided, one-time view.

There were several indicators that changed from the low period (or around seventh grade) to Bubba's sophomore and junior years of high school. The primary subjective indicator that changed was Bubba's level of confidence, both in himself and in his abilities.

It's hard to peg what confidence is and what a loss of confidence is, but Bubba gradually had lost confidence. I think he understood that he was not catching on to math like his peers and he could look around and see other children learning cursive and writing well. He was aware, and over time, it affected him. When he first met the director of the after school math program that he began at the end of seventh grade, she asked him directly if he "had lost his confidence." I was surprised when he answered, "Yes." Not that I hadn't observed it, but that he was so forthright about it. She was experienced with students who had fallen behind, could see it in the objective data and knew the corresponding result – a loss of confidence. A subjective concept and when she made the comment about loss of confidence I knew in my gut she was correct and building that confidence was vitally important.

A year later (in eighth grade) he came home from school one spring day and he smiled his big, healthy smile and said, "Mom, I was the worst one in the class in math at the beginning of the year and now I'm the best." I don't know if it was true that he was the best, but he started getting his confidence back; the smile and the body language said it all. His math teacher even commented on the improvements in Bubba's math and his attitude.

Bubba was generally a man of few words. I eventually learned that if he said he had a headache, he had a headache. He wasn't a faker and he didn't just chatter without a reason. And if he said he had a headache, it meant get the trash can because often a headache was severe enough to cause vomiting. It seemed strange to me that he didn't ask a lot of questions and his responses to my questions were often very short and sweet. Or maybe he would just shrug, or grunt, or say "I don't know." It made it difficult to figure out what was going on during his day at school, if there were any problems, and even what homework was assigned. Comments from the classroom observation portion of his evaluation included "doesn't ask questions."

About the time he started regaining his confidence, more questions started popping out. "What does this button do?" when riding in the car. Or, "What does he mean by that?" in response to a comment during a show we might be watching on television. Or, "What does that word mean?" It sounds odd, but I didn't get many questions for years and years, and then when the questions began again, it was a relief. Various teachers commented that Bubba was raising his hand and participating in class.

As Bubba moved out of elementary school and into middle school, there was a series of behavior issues. He received detentions, and more detentions for missing detentions. He accumulated a couple of in-school suspensions. (Okay, I thought they may have been an over-reaction by the school district.) There were regular emails from different teachers about some in-class behaviors. What was I supposed to do about it, I wondered. I wasn't there in the classroom to see what was happening. Surely there was some logical explanation, right? By the middle of eighth grade, coincidentally about the time he was getting his confidence back, the behavior issues were eliminated. There were no more detentions or suspensions and there were rarely emails regarding behavior.

Other problem areas began disappearing. Assignments were getting written down and homework was getting turned in. By tenth grade, I rarely checked his notebook or book bag for assignments. I thought that tenth grade would be an experimental year, where instead of checking each night to see what Bubba needed to do for that week or the next day, I would leave it up to Bubba. My plan was that if Bubba started flunking classes, I would return to my vigilant prompting and checking. But he didn't start flunking classes and I felt very relieved.

The school district was not crazy about Bubba leaving the resource room and they wanted him to have an aide for some classes in eighth and ninth grade. By tenth grade, Bubba had gone from resource room for reading, writing and math, to no resource room with an aide's assistance, to no resource room and no aide and dramatically reduced prompting and checking at home. And while he wasn't getting mostly As and Bs like he did in seventh grade (when he couldn't write and counted on his fingers), he was getting mostly Cs and some Bs with minimal assistance, while taking physics, algebra, European history and literature.

And there was a subtle change I noticed in the report from NeuroPsych. When he evaluated Bubba in seventh grade, he noted "the presence of a possible emerging anxiety disorder or depressive syndrome that warrants intervention and support." This sentence was eliminated in his evaluation in the tenth grade and replaced with only the comment that Bubba had "some anxiety." Not perfect, but then, are there any high school students who don't have some anxiety?

There were a variety of subjective inputs that supported the objective data along with my gut instincts that we were headed in the right direction. Bubba was smiling more, asking questions, operating relatively detention-free and managing large amounts of his schoolwork without my help. I noticed, his teachers noticed and NeuroPsych noticed. I am not sure that I necessarily chose the best types of interventions that could be done, but I did implement appropriate and effective activities and programs to improve Bubba's academics and his confidence.

Reading Up on Case Law

> *The ultimate question for resolution with respect to this issue, then, is whether the Student's needs are such that without greater levels of 1:1 instruction using the Parent's suggested method of intervention, Student will be deprived of any meaningful education benefit. Again, this is the Parent's burden to prove by a preponderance of the evidence presented at hearing.*[56]

There are a lot of interesting cases I have read, but a couple stood out because of the obvious, but understated, "Mama Bear" quality of the parents involved. In addition, there were applicable components that I found pertinent to our struggle.

This first case I am including, again, reminded me of a Steven King novel in the way it unfolded.[57] The student, a young boy in elementary school, was quite verbal, of a high IQ, and was the recipient of As and Bs in his class work. He was diagnosed with a significant verbal/non-verbal split between his performance and verbal IQ scores. (See Terms and Definitions for more discussion.) By third grade he began to have

---

[56] Before the State Board of Education (State of Ohio), Case No. SE-2183-2008.

[57] Findings of Fact, Conclusions of Law, and Order; Before Linda McCulloch, Superintendent of Public Instruction (State of Montana), OSPI No. 2006-08.

headaches and did not want to go to school. He was identified as needing special education to address social skills and study skills, pragmatic language (addressed with speech pathologist therapy), and motor skill issues (addressed with occupational therapy). Also, he was identified as needing to see the school psychologist, and having adults in the school he would feel safe with, as well as a place to go to decompress.

He continued to struggle; his grades dropped; and he was often bullied or ridiculed by the other students. The school neglected to provide the speech services, counseling for social skills or study skill help; so the parents began providing those services out-of-school and out-of-pocket. It became difficult for the mother to get the student to attend school because he would "throw up in the car in front of the building," or she would have to "pull him into the building," or he would run "after the car" as she left. The problems became so severe that the student said "he wished he was dead," and on "two occasions he tried to jump out of a moving car on the highway on the way to school."

The mother in this case was made of strong stuff. She attempted to work with the school district, educating them about the specifics of her son's condition, providing expert recommendations, providing external therapies, home-schooling part-time, using outside academic programs, and trying medications (under the doctor's recommendations) in an attempt to reduce her son's anxiety. (I would have been tempted at this point to try a few meds myself.)

Middle school was a disaster for this child, compounded by the school district not providing the services identified in the IEP. Representatives of the school blamed the mother for the student's difficulties. After attempting to work with the school district for several years, and essentially, trying to keep their son engaged and alive, the parents (upon expert recommendation) placed their son in a special private school. The parents prevailed in this case receiving around $80,000 to cover a placement in the private school that was familiar with this type of student. They were also reimbursed for the therapies, counseling, outside academic program, transportation and other costs associated with placing him in the school.

The parents filled a Due Process, and in the Due Process the hearing officer found:

- There were several major categories of procedural violations that were determined to result in a denial of FAPE (free and appropriate education). This included not considering evaluation results in the IEP, not producing the IEP in a timely fashion, failure to provide written notice, and failure to allow for meaningful participation of the parents.

- Parents asked for an adult to be available for the student, a smaller class size, an aide, assignments to do at home because of the difficulty to get him to attend school (all in line with the expert's recommendations) – all of which were ignored by the school district. This is a failure of the district to provide written notice, a process that requires thoughtful explanation and data to support the denial of the parent's requests.

- Even though the student was experiencing increasing struggles, anxiety, and failing grades, the district kept the placement "substantially the same" and indeed "cut services," particularly in the student's speech and language/pragmatic language and social skill areas. The hearing officer commented that "parents are not required to stand by and watch while a school system implements the same IEP that has provided no educational benefit in the preceding year."

The parents rejected the last IEP and placed their son in an appropriate setting where he began to make significant progress; he was able to participate in school activities and do his school work. Because the parents successfully proved a denial of FAPE and provided an appropriate alternative, the hearing officer commented that he had "broad discretion to grant appropriate relief, including not only prospective relief, but also retroactive reimbursement for all expenses that the parents incurred because of the failure to develop or implement an appropriate IEP."

This appears to be a case where the parents really tried to work with the system, tried to do the right things for their son and garnered independent input to gauge the appropriateness of their actions. It was obviously not a "good fit" of student to school, and when a child's anxiety level reaches such a level that he is suicidal, it is past time to stop messing around and take it seriously. It is heartbreaking to read about how the process broke down, and astounding to read what the parents went through.

Another interesting case is a situation that is a little happier in the sense that the hearing officer commented that "all parties in the student's life seem to take their responsibilities seriously and carry out their duties professionally."[58] He commented about the parents, that they were "very strong advocates for the student to receive all the meaningful benefits to which he is entitled," and also that the student was very "fortunate."

Note: It is considered a good thing to be a strong advocate in the eyes of the hearing officer.

Note also: The student is fortunate because of that. I know sometimes I have been intimidated or afraid to ask questions or press for data or services, and yet to the hearing officer, this is an admirable quality, being able to advocate.

In this case, the student is identified as a unique learner. The parents privately placed the student in a school that used a specific method to teach reading. (This was apparently paid for out-of-pocket or with money from a previous settlement.) On that method, the student made good progress and the parents wanted the student to receive that method of instruction going forward. It is not specified in the case what the progress was with and without using the method, but it is important to note that the progress was ***measured***.

The hearing officer works through the argument in steps. First he notes that parents "can not and should not dictate school education methodology." The hearing officer allows for it in this case because of the rate of progress the student made learning to read on the parent's requested methodology "as compared to the rate of progress using earlier education methods." The hearing officer states that by not using the method "to do otherwise would be a denial of FAPE." The hearing officer goes on to insist that the methodology be written into the IEP.

These two cases and others helped me understand issues related to Bubba's education and I began to understand some of the basics of special education law.

The law that deals with the education of special needs children is called the Individuals with Disabilities Education Act or *IDEA* (definitely a

---

[58] The Ohio State Department of Education, Case No. SE 1952, 2006.

cool acronym). Parents are constantly being given a document called *Whose IDEA is It?* And I have often pondered that. The spirit, as it is called, of this law is admirable and I do respect the amount of work and discussion that must have transpired in the creation of the law. My understanding is that this law evolved because the children who were in special education back in my day, were really not afforded a "basic floor of opportunity" as it is called. The law was crafted to enable better services for educationally disabled children who were likely not given the minimum services, or any individualized services to address their specific needs.

For parents it is important to get the appropriate service for the child. This may take advocating and providing the services out-of-pocket, but if they are appropriate (which may take expert opinion), reimbursement can come later. If the IEP lists services and they are not provided by the school, the parents should get the documentation to show that the services were not being provided, and the parents should provide those services, if at all possible.

Getting the documentation to prove that services are not provided is tricky. I personally requested the occupational therapists log from the occupational therapist and future District Coordinator 4 both verbally and in writing (received about one year after I requested it), requested the logs from the math computer program the district attempted (received about three months later), and requested logs from the writing tutor they provided (received about two months after request). Each request required multiple written reminders and I would send a request about once a month.

It is likely that the services listed in the IEP are the minimum that the child needs to get an appropriate education, which is referred to as a "basic floor of opportunity."[59] This is very likely much less than what the parents desire as the parents are inclined to want to maximize their child's potential, so the parent's idea of special education is likely much more than what is required by law. Under the law[60], if the services determined by the team result in adequate progress towards the IEP

---

[59] See Board of Education of the Hendrick Hudson Central School District vs Rowley, 458 U.S. 176, 1982.

[60] See 34 CFR 300.320

goals, then the IEP is appropriate. The services provided by the public school system do not have to provide maximum progress, or great progress, or anything resembling the progress the parents may have in mind.

It is admirable to advocate and work with the school district. It can be a fight in the sense that the school district may resist providing services or resist writing services into the IEP. It is not easy and may not be worth the struggle in some ways because there is lost work time, lost sleep, frustration, and stress. For some, it could be easier to find a private school or hire tutors and avoid the battle. For me it was a matter of principle. I paid my taxes that funded education and special education. It was supposed to be free and appropriate, so I decided to take on the battle. It certainly is not for everyone.

Complaint Strategy

> *Parents who are not offered services and supports in inclusive general education contexts for their children with significant disabilities often resort to Due Process, mediation, and even relocation to alternative school districts in order to obtain such experiences for their children.*[61]

I am including this chapter to document the complaint strategy I used regarding Bubba's education. The strategy was code-named *Operation Bury Them in Paperwork*. The letters can't be rearranged to form a catchy word and it is not the coolest acronym, but it accurately describes my approach.

Under *IDEA*, a group of individuals from the school, the parents and possibly other people, form a team to determine the special educational needs for the child. This team is called the Individual Education Program team or IEP team (not such a cool acronym). I haven't met anyone who enjoys these meetings, but they could be out there. The reason the meetings can be uncomfortable range from parents being intimidated, teachers being busy, administrators sitting through meeting

---

[61] Diane Lea Ryndak, Jill Frenchman Storch and David Hoppey, "One Family's Perspective of Their Experiences with School and District Personnel Over Time Related to Inclusive Educational Services for a Family Member with Significant Disabilities," *International Journal of Whole Schooling*, 4 (2), 2008.

after meeting, and there can be disagreements among team members as to what services are appropriate for the child.

It is the latter issue regarding disagreements on what was appropriate for Bubba that led me to trying to understand the idea of *IDEA*. If a child is several levels below grade on a subject, it seemed like a no-brainer to me that either the child is not capable of performing at grade level, or he is capable of performing at grade level. And if he is capable of performing at grade level, it might be a simple, practical technique that brings him to grade level, or it might take methods so complicated and expensive that it is simply not practical. I am sure there are ranges of simple to complicated, and that is where a team has to make the call on what is appropriate.

We focused on reading, writing and mathematics, the old three Rs for Bubba. With Bubba several grade levels behind in math, and being a practical parent, I began providing a simple, uncomplicated tutoring program for him. Grade level gains were two to three levels per year with tutoring. Members of the team, consisting of public school employees, deemed that tutoring was not appropriate. Even after mediation, where agreement was reached for tutoring, the services were not provided. Even after witnessing the dramatic changes in math skills, the school district administration refused to acknowledge that tutoring was appropriate and effective.

So I had found a simple, inexpensive method that was effective for Bubba, but was deemed inappropriate. The very nature of the method being inexpensive made the disagreement process unattractive, because to take a case, called Due Process, to the State Department of Education generally required an attorney. In other words, it is just not cost effective to hire an attorney whose fees are likely to be more expensive than the tutoring.

My first call to an attorney (after an extensive process of just trying to locate one) was disappointing in that the attorney wanted a fifteen thousand dollar retainer upfront, an amount that would cover the cost of tutoring for eight years. I decided that a strategy for arguing for the payment of the tutoring was necessary, but this strategy would need to be implemented without an attorney.

Besides a Due Process, there are other complaint mechanisms that parents can use. I began my complaint process with a request for mediation to the State Department of Education when Bubba was finishing seventh grade, at the time when I initially began providing him the tutoring. I expressed my concerns about the dropping standard scores in mathematics and writing and his lack of passing the state mandated standard tests. After two days of discussions in the mediation with the school district personnel that was overseen by a state-provided mediator, it was agreed that Bubba needed tutoring for math and writing. The district offered to provide the tutoring using a computer-based mathematics tutoring software, and a teacher for the one-on-one writing two hours per week.

With enough experience in bureaucracy, it came as no great surprise that the school district forgot to provide the writing tutoring and gave up mid-year on the computer-based mathematics tutoring. This is why I engaged in another dispute process – the Formal Complaint.

When I filed my first complaint I was very nervous, but I felt that Bubba was getting short-changed. Much scurrying by the district commenced as they attempted to address the complaint. This included lying to the State, lying to Ex and me, and additional law-breaking activities on their part that would later provide additional Formal Complaint, and Due Process material for my strategy. But what I learned most, a big lesson, during this first complaint was that if a request, discussion, or response was not in writing, *it didn't happen.*

"A parent or eligible student may file a written complaint regarding any alleged violations of the *IDEA* Act."[62] My strategy to go to Due Process was preceded by filing a series of State complaints where sometimes the school district was found in violation of the law, and sometimes they were not.

As an example of a common violation, it was a regular occurrence for teachers to participate in part of an IEP meeting and then get up and leave to go back to class, or for some other reason. This is in violation of *IDEA*.[63] By the beginning of high school I was very frustrated with them

---

[62] Margaret C. Jasper, *The Law of Special Education* (Dobbs Ferry, New York: Oceana Publications, Inc., 2000).

[63] *IDEA* 2004. Part 300 Section D.300.321(e)(1) – "A member of the IEP Team described in paragraphs (a)(2) through (a)(5) of this section is not required to attend an IEP Team meeting, in whole or in part, if the parent of a child with a

leaving and so as teachers began excusing themselves in the tenth grade IEP meeting, I had them sign out with the date and time. This is an example of a procedural violation that I was sure of and after filing it with other violations, the practice of teachers leaving meetings early came to a complete stop. In the eleventh grade IEP meeting, one teacher casually looked at her watch, announced she had a doctor's appointment and stood up to leave. District Administrator 4 quickly chimed in, "Sit down." Because the practice of leaving early was so common, it was clear to me that the teacher had no idea why she was summoned to sit, but she sat back down and stayed reluctantly.

By the time I filed the first Due Process, there was a trail of documentation with incidents of services not provided, procedural violations, ignored parent requests, and objective measurements of the appropriateness of the out-of-school program. There was documentation that members of the school district felt the program was appropriate in the form of the meeting minutes, and even e-mails from several of Bubba's teachers. I kept Bubba in "The Program" because it was an appropriate methodology; he was committed to the nightly practice; and he had improved his skills and confidence. I did so knowing that I might not get reimbursed for the costs of "The Program." I don't know how a Due Process hearing would have gone if the process went that far, but I felt that I had prepared as well as I possibly could.

The massive file of documentation, including findings from the State Department of Education, became the memory for the system. The file included every IEP, every test score, relevant emails, each complaint and each response. My file, contained all the facts pertinent to Bubba's educational life, and was more complete and better organized than the files maintained by the district. The overstuffed briefcase containing the

---

disability and the public agency agree, in writing, that the attendance of the member is not necessary because the member's area of the curriculum or related services is not being modified or discussed in the meeting.

(2) A member of the IEP Team described in paragraph (e)(1) of this section may be excused from attending an IEP Team meeting, in whole or in part, when the meeting involves a modification to or discussion of the member's area of the curriculum or related services, if--
(i) The parent, in writing, and the public agency consent to the excusal; and
(ii) The member submits, in writing to the parent and the IEP Team, input into the development of the IEP prior to the meeting."

file, and thus the complete memory, was intimidating to school district representatives by the time I filed my first and subsequent Due Process. It is not surprising, looking back, that they settled both requests quickly and interrupted my strategy by settling the third Due Process before I was able to take action. I had finally gotten properly prepared and organized.

During the Formal Complaint process, there is no involvement with attorneys. Because I was unsure at times, I included possible violations (for example, a district holding an IEP meeting without the parents present, even after parents requested rescheduling the meeting) in conjunction with violations that I was sure were violations, such as teachers leaving the meeting after fifteen minutes (I made them sign in writing that they did), or not providing written notice when they refused our request for tutoring services.

When a parent files a complaint and the State Department of Education investigates the complaint, the school district must respond to the complaint in writing. As part of this process, they must present facts relevant to the complaint. As a result of filing complaints I had indisputable documentation of the facts, many times presented by the school district, and a method for getting facts documented on the State Department of Education letterhead. This process provided data to support my planned Due Process claim, as some portions of the complaints were "fishing expeditions" I initiated to get them to cough up data. In addition, filing complaints caused a large amount of paperwork generation by the school district at a cost of paper and stamps for me. I became somewhat merciless in the sense that I generally filed a complaint around the beginning of summer vacation or winter break when school district personnel were ready to take their time off.

Rather than jump rapidly into the process of Due Process, I wanted to get my feet wet with a small Due Process. My initial Due Process involved a very small issue that included only the tutoring for one summer with a request for reimbursement of less than two hundred dollars. Less than the cost of an attorney for one hour, I believe. I felt that, depending on the outcome of the first Due Process, I would continue on, or learn my lesson and give up.

When I filed the first Due Process, the State again mandated a resolution session, where it was hoped that the parents and the school district could come to an agreement. I organized my documentation for the resolution session around the following four topics:

- U – Unique
- R – Regression
- A – Appropriate
- V – Violations

I had hoped that the first three topics would be sufficient, and wasn't expecting to have to deal with the fourth.

Of course, my thinking was backwards. Wouldn't the fact that Bubba was a unique learner (one in one thousand), who required specific and effective methods, combined with a demonstrated regression prior to implementing the effective method, combined with double grade level gains using the effective (and appropriate) method be enough? No. The resolution session dragged on until I started addressing the violations that had been committed in the non-implementation of the summer tutoring. The completeness of the documentation of the violations was the winning point in the resolution session – not the other three ideas of unique learning style, regression of scores over time, or appropriateness of the tutoring.

Because the first Due Process was settled quickly, with no attorney involvement during a resolution session, I decided to proceed, full speed ahead. The second Due Process was set up to cover the next year of tutoring. The amount was approximately two thousand dollars (the cost of an attorney for roughly eight to ten hours). Formal Complaints and Due Process requests do not have to be bundled together, but there is a two year statute of limitations on filing a Due Process.[64] There is also some point where the parents might be considered to be harassing a school district by filing frequent complaints or Due Process requests, but probably not when they are filing complaints with valid violations of the law and settling or winning their Due Process cases.

I filed the second Due Process about two months after the first, mostly to give myself time to calm down and prepare a complete strategy. By the second Due Process, I was dealing directly with Assistant District Superintendent who was sufficiently brainwashed to use the term

---

[64] See 34 CFR 300.507.

"unique" to describe Bubba. I knew when she started using that term the first Due Process was successful (besides getting tutoring reimbursed).

This meeting (mandated resolution session) took place on a snow day when the students were kept home due to excessive snowfall. I drove to the administration building, which was not far from home, and Assistant District Superintendent met me at the door to the building in order to unlock it. The building was otherwise empty of personnel and we went to her office to discuss the second Due Process. She appeared quite irritated with me by this time as *Operation Bury Them in Paperwork* seemed to be taking its toll, or maybe it was just winter taking its toll. I felt like a pesky fly and her demeanor suggested I bug off quickly.

We skipped over the regression portion of my earlier argument. My argument was primarily about appropriateness. Not so much that the program I had enrolled him in was appropriate – the data clearly supported that. What I focused on, was whether tutoring was appropriate during his ninth grade year at all. The district and parents had agreed during the eight grade mediation that tutoring was appropriate for both writing and math (after a two day intensive negotiation process). They had forgotten to do the writing tutoring and had trouble implementing the computer-based math tutoring they wanted to try. My argument was really focused on what had changed, as they perceived, such that he didn't need the tutoring services anymore.

It took about three iterations for the idea to sink in, but finally the Assistant District Superintendent grabbed her pen and paper and said "I need to find out. Can you say that again?"

Sure. "What expert, or what data do you have; what evaluation at the beginning of ninth grade do you have that shows Bubba didn't need the tutoring anymore?" I asked. "Because you don't have any such data, evaluation or expert opinion," I added.

Indeed, their own independent expert had recommended the writing tutoring. My point was that tutoring services cannot be unilaterally dropped by the school district without prior notice and agreement by the IEP team. This agreement never happened.

I didn't want to completely skip over the appropriateness of "The Program" in the discussion. I told her I needed to get something from my car and trudged out through the snow to pull three years worth of tutoring documentation from my trunk. I sat back down in her office with the crate full of papers and pulled several years worth of IEPs out of my briefcase. I showed her the math goals, of two digit by two digit multiplication. I showed her the writing goals. I showed her how the exact same goals were repeated in each IEP, year after year. I then began pulling the tutoring documents that I had ordered, by date, out of the crate.

"First month – addition and subtraction."

"Second month – addition, subtraction and multiplication."

"Third month – addition, subtraction, multiplication and division."

And so on I went while she sat there stunned. I probably appeared possessed; I know I felt possessed. I was dedicated to getting her to understand the commitment Bubba had made to improve his skills and the efficiency of the direct instruction method used by "The Program." I wanted her to understand that not only was tutoring appropriate, but the method used was appropriate. She sat through my entire presentation of all three years worth of documents, where it was evident that Bubba had not only conquered addition, subtraction, multiplication and division, but he had also mastered fractions, factoring, pre-algebra and algebra.

"Six months and he was successfully performing two digit by two digit, three digit by three digit, single digit division, double digit division and triple digit division. This your staff could not accomplish in three years!" I exclaimed.

"Well," was all she immediately said. I have no idea what she thought. I hoped I had made my point. She indicated that she needed to "find out some things" from her staff.

So the resolution session ended with no resolution and we agreed to engage in mediation. I requested that all statements be backed up with documentation, that each party could be heard for fifteen minutes uninterrupted, and that the district be prepared to make an offer, or it would be a short meeting. I felt very, very nervous but the strategy succeeded again.

Specially Educated

The second Due Process inspired the district to bring out an attorney to represent the school district. Apparently, I had either started getting on the school district's nerves or had crossed some dollar limit. Oddly enough, while this Due Process didn't settle in the resolution session, it did settle in the subsequent mediation session. Indeed, the school district anticipated that I would file a third Due Process by this time and settled that one before I could even file it. A summary of the *Operation Bury Them in Paperwork* strategy is shown in the next figure.

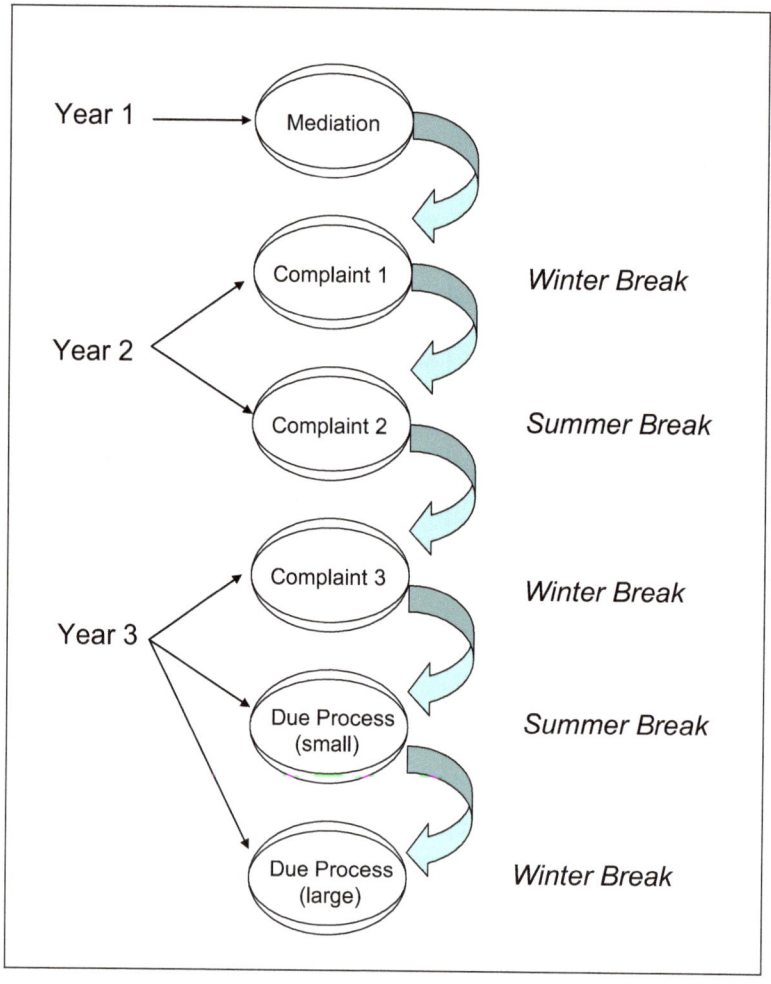

Operation Bury Them in Paperwork

The *Operation Bury Them in Paperwork* strategy consisted of:

- Request Mediation – We met to address unresolved issues in math, writing and more; this was where tutoring was initially agreed upon.

- Complaint 1 – Known violations plus additional possible violations filed as school personnel were ready to take their two week winter break.

- Complaint 2 – Known violations plus additional possible violations filed as school personnel were ready for summer break.

- Complaint 3 – Known violations plus additional possible violations filed as school personnel were ready for winter break; this completed documentation in preparation of what I thought I needed for the planned Due Process, with much of the documentation on State Department of Education letterhead.

- Due Process Small – Initiated to test the waters.

- Due Process Large – Well documented with violations, lack of IEP services and appropriate parent provided services.

I wanted the Assistant District Superintendent to know I was not going away and that I had Bubba's best interest at heart. I used the complaints to build written documentation and to feel out the process. I timed my complaints and Due Process requests such that they were initiated at the worst possible time for the school district employees and the best possible time for me. I never indicated to the school district personnel that I had any kind of plan.

Statistical Note on Complaints

New York City - In a report regarding the New York City school systems special education complaints (a district with 20-something percentage proficiency for their special education students in math and English), it was noted that the complaints revolved around several issues including:

- Not following the IEP.
- Copies of IEPs not provided to the individuals who were supposed to provide services.
- Teachers signing IEPs who were not in IEP meetings.
- Failure to hire the professionals for the student's services for one-on-one support.
- Under-servicing students who were supposed to receive occupational therapy or physical therapy.

These problems were traced to several factors including:

- Failure to report data regularly and publicly.
- Failure to hold schools accountable for not implementing the IEPs.[65]

---

[65] Testimony of Carmen Alvarez before NYC Council Education Committee, Vice President for Special Education at the United Federation of Teachers (UFT), January 2009.

Layman's Interpretation of the Law

Special education law is complicated and confusing.[66]

Just as it is important to understand the language of the law, it is important to understand how the law works. One of the best ways to obtain this understanding is through case histories.[67]

I have read hundreds of Due Process summaries from different states across the United States. What I have found is that there are consistencies and inconsistencies. The inconsistencies are largely differences in hearing officers' interpretations of the law as it may apply to a particular instance, depending on the state. That is my opinion based on my readings. What is fairly consistent are the general rules that hearing officers apply to the Due Process cases.

The law is fair in its intent, but makes it difficult for parents who are trying to get much needed services for their children. A repeated and

---

[66] Margaret C. Jasper, *The Law of Special Education* (Dobbs Ferry, New York: Oceana Publications, Inc., 2000).

[67] Inge N. Dobelis, Editor, *Reader's Digest Family Legal Guide* (Pleasantville, New York: West Publishing Company, The Reader's Digest Association, Inc., 1981).

disturbing finding from my reading of many summaries is an ongoing struggle by concerned parents as their child slips farther and farther away academically, only to be met with resistance by their school district. Histories provided in these cases document year after year of a child falling behind while beginning to show more and more behavior problems. I suppose that these are the types of cases that would go to Due Process as the parents become frustrated and start to see a dim future for their child because educational needs are not met.

Chevy, Not a Cadillac – The IEP should be designed to provide a "meaningful educational benefit" gauged in relation to the potential of the child at issue. The IEP does not need to maximize the potential of the student, and should be reasonably constructed to provide the child with some meaningful benefit. The IEP should have specific, measurable goals. To get a specific methodology for their child, the parent must prove that a school district has failed to design a program that provides a meaningful educational benefit. Parents rarely have been able to argue successfully that a specific methodology should be used. If the school district has a method that will provide more than a minimal educational benefit to the child, then the hearing officer will probably support the school district's choice. It is only when a particular method provides so much improvement, compared to another, that it may be deemed that a particular methodology is appropriate. "The court rules in support of mainstreaming, but determines that educational methods are the responsibility of the state and local education agencies and that parents have no right to dictate specific program or methodology to the school."[68]

Experts – It is recommended that parents get an outside evaluation of their child. It is worthwhile to find an expert who is respected by the school district and who can come to the school and participate in the programming. While the district may not use any of the information provided by the expert, it becomes problematic for the district if ignored, once a complaint or Due Process is filed. Regardless, a good expert will provide a series of recommendations that will help the parents determine how to prioritize requests for their child. The hearing officer considers the qualifications of experts that parents bring forward.

---

[68] Arlene Sacks, *Special Education: A Reference Handbook* (Santa Barbara, California: ABC-CLIO Inc., 2001).

Least Restrictive Environment (LRE) – Moving a child to a private school involves moving him to a more restrictive environment than the public school. When a district pulls a student out of a general education class and places him in a resource room, they are moving the student to an even more restrictive environment. It is the child's right to be placed in the least restrictive environment unless it is shown that it is too disruptive or the child cannot receive educational benefit in the general education classroom. The least restrictive environment should always be the first placement, not the resource room or a private school for learning disabled children. To get a private placement at public expense, the public school must be shown to be an inappropriate placement for the child or violations of the law must be fairly severe. Parents need to notify the school of their placement request in writing in advance, giving the school district time to revise the IEP and possibly re-evaluate the child. The placement selected by the parents must also be appropriate.

More Than Procedural Violations – Procedural violations do not necessarily warrant relief. There may be several issues with how a student's IEP was designed and implemented, but that does not necessarily mean that it constitutes a denial of a free and appropriate education (FAPE). The violations must be proven to have caused substantive harm to the child or the parents. This means that the child lost an opportunity to learn or the parents were impeded from participating in the learning process. Violations do not mean that the district did not take the parents advice or recommendations. If the district listens and lets the parents participate, they can proceed as they wish, unless the parent can provide expert recommendations that contradict, or perhaps better, overpower the course that the school district wishes to take.

Appropriate – Even if there has been substantive harm to the child or parents, relief will not necessarily be provided to the parents. Compensatory education may be provided to make up for previous harm. In our case for Bubba, we tried to prevent harm and provided the compensatory education with an out-of-school program. It is not a given that reimbursement would have been provided in a hearing, even if the substantive harm was proven (such as not providing IEP services). The services we provided needed to be shown as appropriate. The services we provided needed to be tied to his special needs, which were writing and math, and needed to provide educational benefit. It would be impossible to show benefit without measurements of progress.

The Plaintiff has the Burden of Proof – The plaintiff is usually the parent. A parent can not prove anything without documentation in the form of letters, meeting minutes, reports, IEP documents, progress reports, grade cards, and the list goes on. If it was not written down, it did not happen.

Working with the System – A hearing officer will take into consideration whether or not the school district has attempted to work with the family. Likewise, the hearing officer will take into consideration whether or not the family is working with the school. Parents should not shut down in frustration, but stay focused on their goals for the child. A parent needs to write down and document points of disagreement, but continue to work with the school.

In Bubba's case, I began preparing for Due Process when we requested mediation. It was not that I wanted to go to Due Process, but I was willing to proceed to Due Process if necessary. I truly believe that a child who learns differently has the right to be taught how to read, write and do math at grade level, particularly if the child is capable, and at no additional cost to the parents. What we had at the end of seventh grade was a son who was counting on his fingers, unable to write cursive, unable to print legibly, below grade level in reading and very low on confidence. In spite of these deficits, he was getting all As and Bs, and spending a lot of time in the resource room, a place he despised. It didn't seem unlikely that he would get frustrated and drop out of school or begin finding ways to avoid going to school. I requested mediation at that time and began a consistent process of documenting everything because the *parent has the burden of proof.*

I immediately got a tutor for Bubba and began teaching him cursive at home. The tutor recommended an out-of-school program for his math skills. I did not wait to provide a program one minute longer, or consider whether or not the school would reimburse me. I evaluated the program, its documented results, the providers of the service, and weighted the tutor recommendation highly as she was a former teacher and had spent considerable time working with Bubba. Would she testify in a hearing? I wasn't sure of that, but I was sure that I was getting Bubba an *appropriate* program.

After I filed my first complaint, the school district held an IEP meeting without Bubba, Ex or me present. While we had successfully extracted

Bubba from the resource room, the district decided in the IEP meeting that to provide writing services for Bubba, he would need to be moved back to the resource room. I was furious. I would not sign this IEP, of course because I knew they could not move him into a *more restrictive environment* without my permission, but asked for minutes from the meeting where we were excluded. In those minutes, someone had stated during the meeting that the program the parents were providing seemed to "address Bubba's basic skills." The opposite of what they would say when we were present, so I added that to my file. I requested another IEP meeting and attended five IEP meetings that year, not because I liked the meetings but I wanted it to be apparent that I was working *with the school district*. I didn't agree with them, but was willing to continue to work with them.

I wrote on the back of several of the IEPs about the items I disagreed with. This was a shock to the IEP team the first time I did it, but they started getting used to it after a while. I got smarter over time and took the IEP home with me and drafted a type-written list of issues with supporting charts and facts. This got attached to the IEP. The charts clearly showed how, after enrolling Bubba in the out-of-school program, he moved from one-half grade level gain per year, to two grade level gains per year. The methodology used in the out-of-school program improved Bubba's learning rate by a factor of four. Would it be considered a *Cadillac* at a couple thousand dollars per year?

Each complaint that I filed contained procedural violations I was sure of, and others I was not completely sure of. The State Department of Education found that some of these violations were valid and some weren't. Regardless, I knew that *procedural violations alone were not enough* to prove that "The Program" was the right type of special education for Bubba, but that was not the sole purpose of the process of filing the complaints. To respond to the complaints, the school district was required to provide documentation to the State, and consequently a complete paper trail evolved.

"Flowers"

Part 4 – On Toward Independence

There were several years where I was involved with disagreements with the school district, and meanwhile Bubba was moving through his teen years and high school. The beginning of high school was the first time he was freed from the resource room educationally, and by the time he was in eleventh grade he was aide free, taking college preparatory classes, and completing most of his work with few interventions at home. We attempted driving with little success, but meanwhile Bubba passed all his graduation tests, finished up his course requirements, and was handed a "real" diploma, shortly before his eighteenth birthday. Then we attempted driving again and other activities to help move him towards independence.

Teen Years

> *In addition to the stress and frustration they felt while advocating for changes in educational services, the family reported continued experience with school-related stress and frustration after obtaining services for their family member in inclusive general education classes. This family's stress and frustration, however, was related directly to teachers' lack of professional preparation on multi-level curriculum and instruction in inclusive general education classes, as well as school and district administrators' resistance to changing the services they provided for students with significant disabilities.*[69]

Probably the most confusing time in Bubba's life for me was the teen years. He didn't seem as confused as I was. The transition into middle school and then high school is traumatic for any kid. What's cool and what's not.

Teenagers have voice changes, skin changes, growth changes and hormone changes. Hair starts growing in new places and moods can go

---

[69] Diane Lea Ryndak, Jill Frenchman Storch and David Hoppey, "One Family's Perspective of Their Experiences with School and District Personnel Over Time Related to Inclusive Educational Services for a Family Member with Significant Disabilities," *International Journal of Whole Schooling*, 4 (2), 2008.

sour. Why this should happen while Mom was approaching menopause is some kind of sick joke. Mom was having her own skin changes, hair changes and mood issues.

What was most confusing though, was ferreting out learning difference issues from normal teenage issues. There were some behaviors that were easy such as melting down as homework levels increased and dealing with social ostracizing. Well, even the last might not be clear, but it was easy to understand that two and three hours of homework, with extensive handwriting involved would directly lead to frustration meltdown. His brain was exhausted and his hand hurt.

More difficult were other behaviors, such as not turning in homework. Was he forgetting to turn homework in, because that didn't seem to be uncommon among teens. There were occasions when I asked him about turning in homework and he either didn't think it was important or thought that if it was late it didn't count.

Writing down assignments was another issue that seemed to be a tactic to avoid doing homework. If it wasn't written down then it didn't need to be done, right?

On the flip side, I was pretty sure that smart-aleck comments, farting and grunt answers were normal teenage boy behaviors. Wanting Mom to read to him each night was probably not too normal. Taking the book at night and reading to Mom instead was probably not that normal either, but a definite improvement.

So after middle school and ninth grade, even with some confusion, Bubba began emerging with more solid academics, a couple of friends, a bit of work experience by volunteering and an understanding of himself as a laid back, honest and nice person. He loved his religion and video games. He had no use for a girlfriend and said he wasn't ready yet. He became a good tennis player and mastered the art of budgeting his lunch money. He understood his difficulties with diagrams and graphs, and identified himself as a verbal learner, requesting help when needed, as least more than he had in the past.

Bubba had no use for booze, drugs, sneaking out, fights, partying, destroying property or stealing the family car for a joyride. (I would have thought those were completely normal considering the activities my brothers and I participated in as teenagers.) He seemed to be moving at a slower pace than normal in undertaking the rebellious teenager behaviors and was so opposite what I would have expected in such a fast-paced high technology world. I didn't complain though.

Driving

> *Sharp central vision helps us to see acutely and to manipulate objects. However, to have a good sense of our surroundings, to know where we are in space, we need more than sharp sight. We need good peripheral vision. Keen peripheral vision is a skill we all appreciate when navigating, driving, or playing soccer, and it's also a skill that truly distinguishes the good from the exceptional athlete.*[70]

I seriously doubt that any parent looks forward to teaching their child to drive. I certainly didn't. I also didn't know how much a visual-spatial disorder would affect Bubba's abilities. I decided to attempt some early teaching with the intent of enrolling him with an instructor after I had thoroughly understood any difficulties and had thoroughly corrupted him with my own brand of driving. I had him study the 90-page document that listed all the rules of the roads and take the web-based quizzes that were available.

Like any other topic, I decided to take it in small steps with a lot of repetition. That approach seemed to work for almost anything.

---

[70] Susan R. Barry, *Fixing My Gaze* (New York: Basic Books, 2009).

Our first lesson was getting into the car and putting in the key. Unfortunately, I had an expensive car and the key had to be inserted to move any of the mirrors or other devices. And the key was not a normal key either, but nonetheless, that is how we started. Bubba was to adjust the mirrors so that he could see out the back window and each of the side windows. He did just fine and we got back out of the car. "Lesson over," I proclaimed and let out a huge batch of imprisoned air.

The next lesson was to repeat the first lesson. This time I added the seat adjustment step allowing Bubba to adjust the seat so his feet could reach the pedals without having his knees in his chest. I explained to him about the gas pedal, the brake pedal, and using the right foot for both, and switching back and forth. I felt it was necessary for him to understand that the car he was in now did not necessarily have the same buttons in the same places as his Dad's car, or Grandma's car, or other cars, and that he could get into a car and all the buttons could be in another place. Of course the concept of each car being laid out differently made no sense to him.

The third lesson was a repeat of lesson one and two. Now Bubba knew to get into the car and arrange his mirrors, check out the seat adjustment, find the windshield washer and light controls. He knew how to put in the key as well. We went over the shifting controls and discussed what the difference was between park and neutral. With the car in park, I let him start the car. Then I had him turn the car off and felt comfortable that the lesson was sufficient. A little at a time.

For the next lesson, we started with the car in the street, pointing westward at nothing in particular. I hoped that there would be no cars or traffic. We reviewed all the lessons so far; he started the car; and I told him he could try driving around the block. He went pretty slow, but had a tendency to look out the side window of the car. "Look out the front," I told him. He came to a stop sign and stopped and maneuvered around the block just fine. It wasn't so bad, but I didn't let him put the car in the garage. "Just leave it here on the street," I said. The garage was a tight squeeze and I wasn't ready to lose a side mirror.

For the next lesson, we went to the parking lot at the church where there was a lot of wide-open space, no poles, and no other cars. I had Bubba drive around the lot there and pull into a parking spot. He did fine. Then

I had him back the car into the same spot. "Try to put the back bumper as close to the end of the pavement where the grass starts," I told him. "And try to keep the car between the two lines." He did fine with that as well.

During one lesson, he did run the car off the pavement in reverse. The rear wheels were sinking in the muddy grass. Bubba tensed up and he jammed the car into drive and the rear wheels spun in the mud. I asked him to put the car into park because I could see we were about to have a great opportunity for the type of driving lesson he wouldn't get with a paid instructor.

"You are going to learn how to rock and roll," I told him.

"What's that?" Bubba asked nervously.

"You get one chance at this," I explained calmly. I was making a big deal out of the event for some reason. "What you will need to do, is put the car in reverse, let it rock backwards briefly, then quickly put the car into drive and as it begins to roll forward, lightly press on the gas." Bubba was looking even more nervous. To make it very dramatic and I have no idea why, I added, "You will only get one chance at this. Otherwise we will be stuck here all night, so you want to be sure to just lightly press on the gas when we start rolling forward."

He was thoroughly shaken by this point but he put the car in reverse, let it rock backward, roll forward, and got us right back up on the pavement! He managed a fairly complicated maneuver just fine.

Okay. I know. I suppose he was supposed to have his temporary permit before driving the car around the neighborhood.

I wasn't seeing any driving issues due to a visual-spatial disorder. Bubba was able to maneuver the car correctly and did pretty good.

He studied the practice tests for his temporary permit the summer after tenth grade. We reviewed material several times a week, and by the middle of tenth grade we went to the testing station at the Bureau of Motor Vehicles, one of the most horrifying places on earth.

Bubba filled out his paperwork to take the test and proceeded back to a small area that housed about ten computers. Several other teenagers were taking the test that day as well. After about 30 minutes he returned to the waiting area with a slip of paper. Unfortunately, he did not pass his test to get his temporary permit. I was disappointed, and when Ex stopped by later in the week, he was stunned.

"I'll take him down there and he can retake the test. Study the material, Bubba!" Ex said.

We reviewed the material again, and how to take tests. Bubba seemed confused on how to read some of the signs, particularly those with arrows. Ex took him back to the testing center. I was relieved because one visit a year to that place is plenty. Ex called me about an hour later, "No go," he said.

"Ugh," I replied. I wasn't really that surprised. The good news I suppose, was that I was saving an incredible amount of money by not having to provide any vehicle or car insurance for a teenage boy. The bad news was that Bubba did seem a bit humiliated by not being able to pass the test.

Several people made a similar comment, "He just isn't ready to drive yet. That's why he didn't pass." I suppose there was truth to that, so I backed off trying to push him into driving before he was ready.

Graduation

> *The revised regulation includes longstanding United States Education Department policy that a student's right to a FAPE is terminated upon graduation with a regular high school diploma.*[71]

The day was almost here. The class ring was ordered and had arrived as well as the graduation cap and gown. ACT tests were taken; his senior project was completed successfully and with a 90% score. Bubba had completed all his required credits, including four years of English, four years of history, physics, chemistry, biology, two years of Spanish (what? a foreign language?), and four years of math, including algebra, geometry and college algebra. The grade point was not awesome, but he completed the last two years of high school without much prompting from home. And he passed every graduation test required of the seniors – reading, writing, math, science and history. (And they told us it would NEVER happen.)

All that was left was an internship and the graduation signs. Ex was hosting and planning the graduation party and we had our guests invited.

---

[71] Margaret C. Jasper, *The Law of Special Education* (Dobbs Ferry, New York: Oceana Publications, Inc., 2000).

I was almost afraid to invite people for fear that something could go wrong. It had been such a long struggle, for Bubba, myself and Ex.

The last week of school the seniors were required to complete a three day internship in a field that they were interested in. Without a lot of video game developers in our area, we passed on the concept of a video game internship, and instead were able to set up the internship at Bubba's Temple where he could work with the Rabbi. After his first day, Bubba seemed exhilarated with the time he had spent with the Rabbi.

"We went to an unveiling!" He exclaimed.

"What's that?" I'm not Jewish and didn't get the terminology.

"It's a funeral," he said. He actually seemed pleased with the activity, so that was okay with me. Each day I would drop him off at the Temple and he would participate in a variety of activities. Bubba had a great time spending several days tagging along with the Rabbi to charity events, home visits, and speaking engagements.

Meanwhile, I had yet to receive my yard signs. See, I wanted the great big one with his name plastered across it so I could totally embarrass him. Or maybe it was because I was really, really proud. I ordered two signs – one for me and one for Ex, but with only a few days left before graduation had yet to receive them. I furiously exchanged emails with the sales representative.

"Can't find your order," he wrote. I sent him back my saved image of the receipt for the order. By Thursday (two days before graduation) my heart was sinking because it was getting evident that I was not going to get my signs! "I will have a sign made up for you," the sales representative finally conceded.

"Two." I wrote back. "I already have been billed for them!"

When I arrived home from work Friday, the two signs were in the living room. Bubba had picked them up from the sales representative at school. The signs were around two feet by two feet, not nearly the size I had been hoping for. Oh well. I quickly posted my sign in the front yard and gave the other sign to Ex. Likewise, he proudly posted his sign in the front yard at his house.

I expected to be a blubbering fool come graduation day. I don't think I cried a tear, although I may have come close. I dropped Bubba off at the high school three hours before the ceremony so he could ride the bus downtown to the convention center where graduation was to be held. He had his cap and gown and cell phone. I feared that somehow he could get lost and not make the ceremony. I whispered to myself as I drove back home; please get on the bus; please get in your robe; please wear your cap; please get in line (stay there); and please pay attention!

I suppose that deep down, I feared that after years of struggle, failures and successes, it would be too easy to have graduation day go smoothly. I had come to expect roadblocks, misunderstandings, and heroic efforts to achieve what many parents just expected. I was holding my breath, waiting for some unknown tragedy.

I was overwhelmed with all the family support. My two older brothers had come into town from out-of-state the night before, my mother drove down from out-of-town, Ex's mother and husband drove in from out-of-state, and my other brother and his wife attended as well. We all visited a pub together prior to the event (the drink certainly helped my state of mind), and then wandered over to the convention center to the auditorium where the graduation was to be held.

And there they were. Around 300 graduates, and it didn't take long to spot Bubba, perfectly attired and standing in line with his fellow classmates. Hurrah! I felt such relief and was able to confidently find a seat and relax. Our group sat in a row together and it was truly a memorable, wonderful experience. (Okay, maybe the speeches by the 19 valedictorians and the long winded, motivational rants by different administrators were a bit boring.)

Eventually it came time for the students to begin lining up for the receiving of the diplomas. Waiting, waiting, waiting. We had to politely clap for the students whose last names were early in the alphabet.

Mom grabbed her camera and boldly parked herself close to the stage as Bubba's group lined up to the right of the stage. Where was he? Okay, I found him in line. And then it finally did happen. Bubba crossed the stage and received his handshake and his diploma. He graduated!

Big cheer from the Bubba section and a big sigh of relief from Mama Bear.

Driving – Part 2

Every parent knows how crucial the choice of friends is for every child. Childhood friendships tell parents which ways their children are tending. They are important because good friends bring you up, and bad friends bring you down. So it matters who our children's friends are.[72]

We postponed any further attempts at driving until graduation was completed. Our schedule was pretty full up until then and I felt that maybe it would be better to tackle the driving issue once all the graduation activities had passed.

For the three weeks after graduation, I had Bubba begin studying the driving laws again. We reviewed signs, signs that had caused him difficulty on his previous attempts. He read parts of the manual and I quizzed him on those parts when I got home from work each day. He was filling out a lot of employment applications as well, because it was time for him to get a job.

Some of this time after graduation he spent with a friend, a friendship that had developed over the last two years. He was a young man who graduated with Bubba and had graduated with honors. This friend

---

[72] William J. Bennett, *The Book of Virtues* (New York: Touchstone, 1993).

appeared to have some eccentric characteristics and a crazy-smart memory like Bubba. Sometimes he slept over, or they hung out playing video games, or I took them to the movies. This fellow had his driver's license, but was on probation due to a speeding violation while driving with his mother! Whoa!

I don't know if I would call it peer pressure, because Bubba's friend didn't seem to be teasing Bubba about not driving yet. He was actually very encouraging and down-to-earth about the difficulties he had encountered during his own driver's test. He explained that his mother wouldn't let him drive alone yet and she only let him drive when he was with an adult family member. His attitude and all the talk about driving had a positive effect on Bubba. He was ready to go try to get his temporary license again.

I was between contracts in early July of that summer and so it was also a convenient time for me to take Bubba to try it again. We went to the Bureau of Motor Vehicles building and took a number and waited. The room was filled with people of all ethnicities and backgrounds, and was so cold my toes began to freeze up. There was the constant background noise of number calling, chatting, and babies crying. People seemed to meander aimlessly about, sometimes being called to check in and then return to the hard, plastic waiting chairs.

Finally Bubba's number was called and I held my breath while he took his vision test. He passed that test and I put his prism glasses back into my purse. These were the special glasses the vision therapists had prescribed for Bubba to address his convergence insufficiency, the ability of his two eyes to work together. He rarely wore the glasses by this time, generally ignoring their presence, but for some reason I thought he might need them. After the vision test, the attendant pointed him to the computer area where he sat to take the written test for his temporary license - his third try.

I returned to my seat and pulled out my puzzle book. I did several puzzles and got bored. I peeked around the corner and saw Bubba sitting at the computer, not really doing anything. I sat back down and read the different signs posted throughout the waiting area – "No cell phones", "Donate organs", "Authorized Personnel Only", "ID Kids for Safety". I got bored again, peeked around the corner again and saw Bubba staring at the computer again.

After about 45 minutes, he came around the corner shaking his head from side to side. No pass. We picked up his identification documents from the friendly fellow at the counter and left the building. Once in the car, I explained to Bubba that it was okay, we would come back the next day (after the holiday) and try again. I prompted him to remember every question on the test; we marked those areas in the manual; and we wrote notes on the back of the manual for the questions we could not find.

He studied over the weekend while visiting his grandmother out-of-state. He studied in the car on the way home from her house. He studied as we drove back to the Bureau of Motor Vehicles; and he studied while we waited for his number to be called. They called his number and he was sent back to the computer area. Another 45 minute wait and he came meandering around the corner this time with his thumb up. He passed!

I wanted to call Ex to tell him, but Bubba said he would call him when he got home. As soon as we got into the house he grabbed his cell phone and began dialing. But it wasn't his dad that he called; it was his buddy.

"Sea of Flowers"

Part 5 – Reflections

There was a lot of educating going on during Bubba's school years. I look back and am astounded by the number of times I heard the word "Never" and the number of times it turned out to not be true. I received a number of lessons in the process. The way our story unfolded was unfortunately (or fortunately, I am not sure) not unique.

Never? Or A Different Way?

> *"I can't do this. I'll never be able to climb up that hill."*
>
> *And he lifted me up in his strong, gentle arms and said something I will never forget. He said, "I know you can do it. There is nothing that you can't do."*
>
> *He taught me that nothing is impossible.*[73]

I have heard "Never." He will never read, write or be an athlete. At the age of five, it is reprehensible that someone would proclaim "Never." There may be only one entity around that has the all-knowing, all-seeing power of predicting the future, and even that is not known for sure. The regular humans that we know or meet every day do not have the authority to proclaim "Never."

I have heard other examples besides the proclamation made by a school psychologist about my son at the tender age of five, and I am including a masked version of some of the stories.

---

[73] Ted Kennedy Jr. speaking at the funeral mass for his father at the Basilica of Our Lady of Perpetual Help, Boston, August 29, 2009

Specially Educated

An ABD (all but dissertation, PhD student) and respected project manager, declared to me one day at work that he used to ride the "short, yellow bus" in elementary school. He was also valedictorian of his high school class.

A PhD writes, at the age of five, it was determined that she would never be able to attend college. She graduated early in her bachelor's degree program.

A mother writes that their daughter's psychologist told them not to place their daughter in a high-performing school because she would not be able to perform. She is currently in college.

A father writes that their son had a head trauma and they were given a host of "nevers." His son can run, golf, play the trumpet, do karate and is at grade level in math. He says, "We can never say never."

I attended the MBA program at a large university with a co-worker who was a chemical engineer. He informed me one day that he needed to take much longer to study because he was dyslexic. Did he think never?

A father writes that their son was told he could never play sports. He just finished a baseball season, and now is on the football team.

A parent writes how she was told that her son would only to live to the age of six months. He is attending college.

One mother says that she was told her daughter could not take a foreign language and she would never be able to learn Spanish. They were told she would never walk, talk, read or write. She managed two years of Spanish in high school and has continued on in college.

At our last visit with NeuroPsych, he was thrilled with the progress that Bubba was making, particularly in math. This was totally unexpected. He was cautious, and stated as we were finishing our consultation, "He is doing much better, but he will never be an engineer or an architect." I didn't even say anything in response, but gave him my best evil eye. "Okay, Mama Bear," he said, back-pedaling. I think he knew I had an allergy to the word "Never."

Expectation is synonymous with hope. The term "Never" engages low expectations and has the capacity to extinguish or diminish a parent's hope. If the parent's expectations are artificially lowered due to a proclamation of "Never," how are the outcomes for Junior affected? How can a school district professional proclaim "never read, write or be an athlete" to the parents of a seemingly normal five year old boy? And does it sound like an anomaly or some type of rare occurrence if it is so easy to collect stories of "Never?"

And what if it just takes another way of doing things? A common expression in teaching is that the teacher needs to address "multiple learning styles." Take a left-hander and a right-hander – do we teach them the same way? Okay, maybe, but the mechanics of operating many devices has to be taught or learned differently because many devices assume right-handed operation.

In Bubba's first grade class, as I sat observing one day, I noticed that the teacher taught letter writing for the right-handers. I asked her later if she could show the left-handers how to write and she replied to me "I don't have time." And she didn't, as she spent a good deal of class time diffusing the six-year-olds' arguments. She told me that she had "Brianna teaching Bubba how to write." Nothing against Brianna, but she was a six-year-old right-hander, and I felt she was under-qualified.

Using a six-year-old right-hander to teach my six-year-old left-hander wasn't what I had in mind when I was hoping for "out-of-the-box" thinking. That approach, like several others that were implemented by the special education system, stood no chance of defeating "Never."

If it is recognized that there are multiple learning styles, it shouldn't be a stretch to imagine that instead of "Never," maybe the answer is to try teaching the child a different way. And in a way that makes sense.

Educating Family

> *The biggest surprise of all has been that there have been great advantages to having a child who has learning differences. It has added a lot of richness, closeness, and opportunities for self-reflection. It's given our family a chance to look at our values and the values of the world.*[74]

"You kids never did that," was spoken by my mother on more than one occasion, like when Bubba cried for seven hours straight one morning his first week of life. I was exhausted, ran out of gas and Mom took over the process of walking and rocking the baby. I retreated to my bedroom and crashed for several hours. When I awoke later, Mom was laying flat-out on the couch with Bubba sleeping soundly across her chest. Perhaps everyone finally ran out of steam, including Bubba, but Mom managed to handle the situation without me.

Later, when Bubba began having breath-holding spells, and again when he experienced seizures, I heard, "You kids never did that." I can think of a few other instances when I heard the remark, but I won't go into them. Bubba continued to present situations that were apparently unlike those that Mom remembered when raising her children.

---

[74] Dana Buchman and Charlotte Farber, *A Special Education, One Family's Journey Through the Maze of Learning Disabilities* (Da Capo Press, 2006).

One memorable experience for me happened at Myrtle Beach while on a family vacation with my older brother and his wife, step-daughters and grandchildren. Bubba and I flew to South Carolina and met up with my parents there. We stayed with them in their motor home and visited the rest of the group at their rented condominium down by the beach. One of the favorite past times of the kids is to cruise up and down the strip along the beach on scooters. Some folks drive golf carts and decorated carts up and down the beach front, people-watching and looking for friends. At one point, my older brother, Dad, Bubba and two of the other young boys went under the beach house to fire up their scooters for cruising. From the balcony I saw the two younger boys take off down the strip. Shortly after that, Bubba came back upstairs to the deck, followed by my brother.

"He can't ride it," my brother informed me. I had heard the "he can't" a lot by this time. I turned Bubba around and he, Dad and I went back downstairs to the garage area under the deck. We approached a scooter.

"Get on," I said. Bubba expressed some hesitation, but I could tell he wanted to learn how to ride the scooter. My father stood by watching.

"This is the gas." I showed him the lever. "This is the brake. Pull the lever here, to go faster. Pull this one to stop." I had him practice moving the levers several times. I showed him how to start the scooter.

"Now what I want you to do is to pull the gas lever, real slowly so you go forward just a little – then stop using the brake." Bubba did just fine. We repeated this sequence a few times, allowing the vehicle to move further with each repetition and soon he was ready to go. Dad and I went back upstairs and as I looked over the balcony, there went Bubba down the street on the scooter. My brother looked at me and said "Huh." Dad didn't say anything.

It got easier to understand over time. At one point Mom became obsessed with Bubba and shoe-tying. Fine motor skills were definitely an issue for Bubba and I think it can appear that a child is lazy or oppositional when he or she doesn't perform a simple task that children much younger can do just fine. I don't think a child is necessarily lazy or oppositional. He or she may be very aware that their fingers aren't as nimble as the other kids and it is embarrassing to not accomplish tasks that peers are managing to accomplish. Naturally, the child will avoid those tasks, especially in public.

I had spent several years teaching Bubba the simplest tasks and was rewarded with many tears related to shoe-tying, zippers and buttons. Bless Mom because she kept trying when I resigned to purchasing only Velcro shoes, drawstring pants and pull-over shirts.

I have read hundreds of articles, several books, met with other parents, met with the pediatrician, NeuroPsych, every teacher Bubba ever had, but most importantly, I have spent his entire life (less a couple weeks here or there) with him, watching. Watching him play with other children. Watching him watch other children. Watching him eat, sleep, read, play, calculate, run, bike and so on, and teaching a lot of those skills to him. After hours and hours, days, weeks and months over several years and after many tearful shoe-tying attempts, it was no longer a worthy battle for me.

Mom was not going to give up on shoe-tying though, and eventually Bubba was able to tie his shoes, although he would avoid the effort if at all possible. When Bubba gets a new pair of shoes now, he ties them at the point of purchase. The shoes stay tied their entire life, rarely feeling what it is like to be untied. But Bubba can tie his shoes.

Mom took on manners as well, which was a worthy battle. This was a battle I was struggling with and she did a good job. Bubba holds the door open for her, and also for me, especially if Mom is watching. Most recently I found him holding the door for families at the library and cute girls at the movie theater!

My Dad was less successful with Bubba. He was fairly demanding when we were growing up and had high expectations for his children. His approach to Bubba was at times critical and Bubba's reaction was less than favorable. There was a time when Bubba refused to speak to his grandfather, not really being disrespectful, but not wanting anything to do with him either. Over time, Dad became less critical and Bubba changed his approach. I spent some time explaining to Bubba how his grandfather would sometimes "push his buttons" and that perhaps getting upset was only giving his grandfather the response he was expecting.

I will never forget the day he tried a new approach. Dad had attempted to push Bubba's buttons during a visit when Bubba was about twelve or thirteen.

"You know, you aren't doing that right," my Dad commented to Bubba. Bubba looked him right in the eye and with convincing sincerity responded, "Really. That is so interesting." Dad had no response to that and that was the beginning of the end of Bubba's silent treatment of his grandfather. It took a bit of work and a few adjustments on both sides.

My oldest brother lived several states away. Because it was a long drive we only saw him once or twice a year. He would zoom into town, stop by the house, and immediately cruise up to the gaming room to play the latest video games with Bubba. He didn't seem the least bit intimidated by Bubba and didn't seem to treat him any differently from the way he treated his own daughters. Maybe it was easier for him because he had his own children.

I found that educating my family was about being patient with them, teaching them when I could about some of the special characteristics of Bubba and letting them learn on their own that he learned differently. It was also about learning from them and letting them do part of the work, especially when my own methods didn't work, or I found myself tired or frustrated.

As a parent of a child who learns differently, I have had to deal with disappointments efficiently because there can be so many. I have had to grieve those disappointments, but play the cards that were dealt, and appreciate the interesting and valuable lessons along the way. But my extended family, perhaps not as close to the situation, sometimes rejected the notion that there was anything different about my little angel, and didn't have years of experience and education in the matter – indeed they may have not even wanted to acknowledge a difference or an issue. I needed to understand and accept that, because getting upset and frustrated with them was not an effective option. The very people that may not understand a child's differences are the same people the child desperately needs in his life. And I found that sometimes other family members could accomplish the teaching that I could not.

Educating Mom

> *She will never take for granted a spoken word. She will never consider a step ordinary. When her child says 'Momma' for the first time, she will be witness to a miracle and know it. When she describes a tree or a sunset to her blind child, she will see it as few people ever see my creations. I will permit her to see clearly the things I see – ignorance, cruelty, prejudice – and allow her to rise above them.*[75]

The most special part of special education can be the education of the parents. We learn about disabilities, psychologists, limitations of our children, the law, bureaucracies and their inefficiencies, and how to teach our children better at home. We change and turn into people we never thought we would be and learn to tolerate more than we could have thought imaginable.

I had a "normal" childhood where learning came easy, friends came easy, athletics came fairly easy and other activities, such as playing an instrument or learning a foreign language came easy. I was not properly educated for the job as Bubba's mother. I didn't have fine motor issues,

---

[75] Erma Bombeck, *Motherhood, The Second Oldest Profession* (New York: McGraw-Hill Book Company, 1983).

or problems integrating with other children socially. I didn't have visual-spatial or organization issues. I had never heard of such issues until Bubba collided with the school system.

Ex, the grandparents and I spent several years trying to teach Bubba how to tie his shoes. Constant retraining was needed for hand-washing, tooth brushing, bath-rooming, showers, finding homework assignments, math, writing and the list goes on. It doesn't feel like too many things came easy for Bubba. One lesson I learned was that with patience and consistency he would learn and eventually become responsible for reminding himself to do tasks himself. I sometimes would joke that repetition was key to success in teeth-brushing because by the time Bubba was in eighth grade he was remembering to brush in the morning and in the evening without prompting and it only required about twelve years (we won't count the first year of life) of 365 days, twice a day – around 9000 prompts!

We enrolled Bubba in several recreational league sports including basketball, baseball, football and soccer. He needed physical activity and physical skill building. How depressing when your child spends the maximum amount of time on the bench when he is the child that needs the maximum amount of time on the field.

When Bubba was about eight or nine years old and playing in the little league, I remember asking his baseball coach if Bubba would get a chance to pitch an inning. The coach, a rather rough character, was sitting in front of me on the dugout bench and I was standing behind him. He turned around and looked at me and started laughing, "You've got to be kidding." I wasn't kidding at all. This was little league baseball, not the majors. The message that I received from the coach was that if he put Bubba into the game to pitch, it could jeopardize the team's chance of winning. I returned to the bleachers, very angry and disappointed. I learned that a lot of people have a great desire to see their eight-year olds win the game, and they would easily or unknowingly sacrifice the self-esteem and opportunities of other eight-year olds to achieve that win.

The coach that Bubba had the next year was a completely different animal. He never hesitated to let Bubba pitch part of a game, play third base and play short stop. This coach was totally contrary to the other coach who would only play Bubba the minimum amount, which was the league-required three innings per game. And those three innings were spent banned into right field. The new coach played all the players *and* his team went to the playoffs. I learned that not every coach operates on the principle of playing only their "best" players. Some coaches operate on the model of "you are only as strong as your weakest player." How refreshing.

Of course I came to realize that every time you think things are tough you can look around and find someone who has it tougher. But that doesn't mean we didn't have an uphill climb. Small, normal events were never taken for granted at my house. Bubba might crack a good joke, or walk home with another student from school, or get a "B" in math or make his bed without needing reminding. These would each seem amazing to me because if I thought back to even a few years prior, it would have seemed impossible.

Certain lessons stood out along the way. I remember the third year of baseball when I took Bubba to the first practice in the pony league, or whatever league the kids get into when they get toward middle school. The coach gave us "the look" when we arrived. (I am not being over-sensitive.) He tossed the ball back and forth to Bubba and then asked me if Bubba should be there. It was supposed to be a recreational league and I said "Yes." He told Bubba to go with one of the other players and as Bubba ran ahead, the coach leaned into the other player and told him to "throw it as hard as he could." The other player began whizzing balls at Bubba who caught some of them and missed some of them. Bubba mumbled "geez" and began getting visibly upset. The coach looked to me and I suggested that since Bubba was barely over the age bracket, maybe he could get placed back in the lower level league. I am not sure what I learned that day, other than there are places I guess where he didn't belong. It could get too dangerous. That was Bubba's last year in baseball.

I can remember another day when I sat at the kitchen table with Bubba, helping him with his math from "The Program." He had reached a particularly challenging topic and was getting frustrated. He would begin a problem and then start erasing his answer, eventually ripping the paper and working himself into a frenzy. I began getting upset also; my patience was not always as strong as I needed. I said to him, "You can just quit the program if you want and then you won't have to do this."

He yelled at me, and I mean yelled, "No!" Bubba wanted to learn and I learned to never doubt it after that day. He would not consider leaving a program that was hard for him. He made tremendous progress on that program and he knew it, and it was important to him to catch up. Some situations were just too dangerous to continue, such as baseball, and some activities were too important to Bubba for him to quit.

An important lesson I learned is best depicted in the expression "pick your battles." Boy ain't that the truth. There weren't enough hours in the day to address every issue, and what seemed important to some people, or what may have seemed important to me at one time, sometimes just had to be let go. Priorities had to be established, and some expectations lowered or dropped.

When Bubba was in elementary school, most nights he would take a bath before bed and then I had him get dressed for the morning. Yes, he slept in his clothes. Otherwise, he would have never made it to the bus on time. He didn't start wearing pajamas (I am sure my mother would not want to hear this) until middle school, after he had mastered the art of getting ready in the morning.

Shoe-tying went on the back burner; there were ways around it. Bubba dictated many of his long written assignments while I did the actual hand-writing. Did I want him to do it himself, of course. But two hours of homework would stretch into four hours or more and that just seemed ridiculous. Jeans and shirts that buttoned up, forget it. Too much of a problem if you wait too long to get to the bathroom or have to change clothes for physical education. Hair combing – not going to happen, so get a hairstyle that doesn't need a comb. I could go on. And along the way, there were plenty of people to tell me that I wasn't doing it right, or that I needed to do more.

"Mother knows best" is an old expression. For some reason I have never heard of an expression, "the school district administrators know best" or "the teacher you have for eight months knows best." Having doubts with myself at one point, crying in frustration while on the telephone to a member of the parent's advocacy group, the advocate said, "No one knows your son better than you do." Finding an independent special education advocacy group and reaching out helped me put my role in the proper perspective. I did know best; I just didn't believe it at times. While I wasn't properly educated or trained to be Bubba's mother, I evolved into that position to the best of my ability.

Along with patience, and celebrating the little things, I also received an education in tolerance. This was a needed lesson, and how much less of a person would I be if Bubba was the natural athlete, or natural learner or a natural politician? Would I have been the coach that excluded another special child? Would I have been the teacher who suspended the student for following the directions as he understood them? Would I have laughed at the parent of the quiet child who just wanted to pitch once in a baseball game? Would I have denied basic services to a pupil who could jump grade levels by receiving those basic services? Would I have looked the other way as my child ostracized their neighbor? Perhaps I would have if Bubba hadn't come along.

Educating the School

> *Never pour water on a grease fire and never discharge a fire extinguisher onto a pan fire, as it can spray or shoot burning grease around the kitchen, actually spreading the fire.*[76]

A unique learner. Well, we all are; and it took me eleven years to finally get Assistant District Superintendent to use those three words when referring to Bubba. Why was that important? It is a label that is palatable, descriptive and can be tossed around like "global warming" or "politically correct," and folks have roughly the same interpretation with no specifics necessary. It also accurately described Bubba because I too, began to see less and less of a disability and more ability, given the correct teaching methodology.

After meeting with school personnel in the second Due Process complaint, Assistant District Superintendent expressed noticeable irritation with me. "We have bent over backwards to help Bubba," she spewed. "We tried to add more teaching assistance, but you thought he needed to have swimming class. Swimming!"

When you have shown school personnel the experts' recommendations and they don't get it, the job as parent and advocate becomes more

---

[76] "Stand By Your Pan," National Fire Protection Association, 2008.

difficult. I have nothing against teachers and have met fantastic teachers over the course of Bubba's education, but most of the teachers at Bubba's school were fresh out of college and had never taught a student like Bubba.

Every expert recommended physical activity during the school day, including Bubba's pediatrician, and swimming was considered an excellent choice because it was relaxing, especially for an overwhelmed student. Swimming allows the student with visual-spatial difficulties to relax even more because they are free to move without the fear of tripping, getting hit by something, or running smack into an obstacle they didn't see.

If Bubba hadn't been in swimming in the ninth grade, I feared he would have completely melted down and refused to attend school. He needed the physical activity and a break during the day. Stress relief. Plus, he usually looked and smelled clean after swimming, and his ears and belly button were spotless.

Bending over backwards is not about discarding important recommendations of the parents, the experts and the literature. Bending over backwards is not about ignoring methods that clearly work while choosing the same method that doesn't work.

Each year Bubba got an entirely new set of teachers. I always made it a point to ask if they had ever encountered a student with visual-spatial difficulties, or a verbal learner. A verbal learner generally learns better by hearing instructions out loud, even if they are the one doing the talking. Some people thrive on diagrams and some respond better to words. Not one teacher ever responded "Yes" except for an occupational therapist Bubba had in the ninth grade. Each year I provided a standard write-up from the U.S. Department of Education, if there was an interest. Only one person ever expressed much interest, and that was Bubba's counselor. She read books on the subject of students with visual-spatial disturbances, social issues and other quirky issues. She got the true meaning of "unique learner" and she was a unique counselor.

I presented school district personnel repeatedly with relevant information on how to better address the needs of Bubba, a unique learner, a verbal learner. And year after year, the majority of his teachers and members of the school administration staff ignored the information.

Specially Educated

I couldn't help but think about the school district personnel fighting a grease fire. You tell them to try baking soda and they throw water on it. "We're working really hard!" they claim, but unfortunately the fire gets worse. So you call in an expert fire fighter who says, "Try baking soda." They nod in agreement and throw water on the fire. The fire keeps spreading and now they are working really, really hard!

"Maybe you should get an opinion from your own expert," Mama Bear declares. They call in their own expert who says, "Try baking soda." So they try a little baking soda and a lot more water. The fire is getting dangerous now so Mama Bear pulls out the baking soda and starts tossing it on the fire. The fire is dying out – it gets smaller and more manageable.

They barely notice and fill their buckets with more water.

That's the best way I can describe the process of educating the school about Bubba, a unique learner. A verbal learner. Not the typical fire that they were used to fighting. After eleven years of data, measurements, experts, evidence from Mama Bear, there was barely recognition that it was a different kind of fire.

The System Has No Memory

> *The side of a house isn't a feather pillow either, and a car that has just crashed through one must have sustained major damage, damage that simply couldn't have been repaired overnight. And when he gets there, what does he find?*
>
> *Only Christine, without so much as a ding in her fender.*[77]

There are a lot of systems we all encounter in this life. Government systems, such as the Internal Revenue Service, are systems that we periodically deal with, or retail systems that track what we buy. The grocery store that I frequent sends me coupons on items that I buy in their store because I am a "valued shopper." That system has a memory. My car has a memory system that keeps track of when the maintenance is due, how many miles I have driven, and what my gas mileage was today. The computer I am working on is a system that has memory and storage for files and pictures that I want to keep.

Most of my career I have worked on big computer systems, systems that keep track of inventory, sales, tax or contract data. Most big systems keep history, either because their owners are mandated by law, or the

---

[77] Stephen King, *Christine* (New York: The Viking Press, 1983), 444.

owners are interested in making more money by tracking revenues and expenses over time. Big retail systems monitor the effectiveness of promotions so that marketing can get smarter and the company can make more money.

The biggest system I have encountered so far that has no memory is the education system. Modifications were provided for my son with no justification, and no tracking of their effectiveness. Similarly, with interventions, no measurement of a baseline performance was initiated that included a comparison to performance during or at the completion of an intervention. And therefore, no memory of intervention and modification history escorted my son from year to year.

I found that it was the parent's job to maintain history, request documents and keep files. It was my job to lug around stacks of paperwork to combat useless interventions tried and forgotten in previous years. I attended teacher meetings with the understanding that each new set of teachers had no knowledge of what transpired the previous year, let alone in middle school and grade school.

I am not big on giving out advice. I think every parent in special education is likely to encounter positive and negative experiences. But parents need to maintain the system memory, the files and data because it would not be wise to assume that there is a comprehensive record available and maintained by the education agency. And once again: If it wasn't written down (and you don't have a copy), ***it didn't happen!***

The "High" Cost of Tutoring

> *I have seen so many programs that are society's giveaways: Housing, welfare, special education, free medical care, free transportation, adoption subsidies, social security disability for alcoholics and drug addicts. The list is endless, and the results have not produced a more responsible or productive population. There may be a few isolated success stories paraded by the media, but the whole picture does not justify the billions spent by taxpayers.*[78]

The tutoring used to improve Bubba's "learning disability" in math cost about $1000 per year plus driving to the tutoring center once a week, plus the time involved at home to oversee the work Bubba was doing on a daily basis. This tutoring began at the end of seventh grade. The school district's alternative to tutoring was the resource room where he had supposedly been getting individualized instruction for his math disability since first grade. Then they tried an untested, non-productive computer-based math program that was a dismal failure. When that didn't work, the school district personnel tried to ignore the fact that Bubba needed tutoring.

---

[78] Judge Judy Sheindlin and Josh Getlin, *Don't Pee on My Leg and Tell Me It's Raining* (New York: Harper Collins Publishers, Inc., 1997).

The factor for education costs related to children with the least severe needs, identified as specific learning disabilities, is almost a factor of two. In other words, if it takes $10,000 to educate a child with no disabilities, it takes, on average, $20,000 to educate a child with a specific learning disability. This means that the school district would have about $10,000 per year to apply to the remediation and accommodations for the student's disability (including administration costs).

At Bubba's school district, the resource room with individualized instruction was the only remediation effort for his math disability in grades one through seven. During the eighth grade, he was in the resource room, plus he was receiving the tutoring at home with "The Program." By ninth grade, he was no longer in the resource room, but was back in the general education classroom and still receiving tutoring at home with "The Program." Likewise, in tenth grade he continued with the tutoring and the general education classroom model. The data tell the story about the high cost of tutoring.

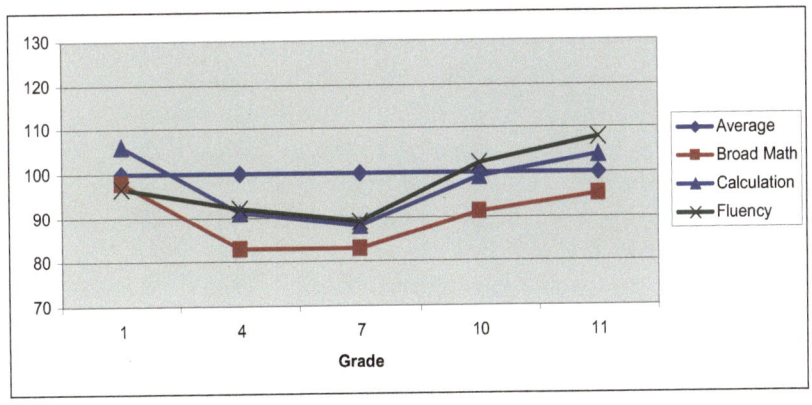

Standard Scores in Math by Grade

During his first seven years, Bubba was rewarded with standard scores that dropped from year to year creating a larger and larger gap between his abilities and the abilities of his peers. While his calculations and math fluency were around normal when he was placed in the resource room, by fourth grade they had dropped to below normal and maintained that drop up through seventh grade.

With tutoring and a subsequent return to the general education classroom, however, the trend was reversed, and after three years of tutoring, the calculations and fluency were back to normal, dragging the math applications along behind. That cost was about $1,000 per year, plus transportation and IEP stress.

Suppose a tutor costs $50 per hour. For $10,000 a district can provide a student 200 hours of one-on-one tutoring to remediate his or her disability. That is about five hours per week during the school year. We paid $30 per hour for a highly qualified math tutor the summer after seventh grade. For $10,000 per year, that would be almost 350 hours, or around 8 hours per week of one-on-one tutoring.

I can only ask why. Why wasn't tutoring provided to Bubba at an earlier age by the experts in public education? Why push a non-working, expensive model? And even after the data were showing remarkable improvements using the tutoring model, why was the answer to try to push Bubba back into the resource room and deny tutoring.

From the ERIC Digests:

> "One-to-one tutoring has long been recognized as superior to group instruction, especially for students with special needs. Tutoring can adapt instruction to the learner's pace, learning style, and level of understanding. Feedback and correction are immediate. Basic misunderstandings can be quickly identified and corrected, practice provided, and more difficult material introduced as soon as the student is ready. Tutoring has emotional as well as cognitive benefits. Students can achieve at their own pace without being compared with faster learners. The extra attention and emotional support may help fill important psychological needs for children from troubled or single-parent families."

Note that the ERIC digests are funded by the Office of Educational Research and Improvement (OERI), of the U.S. Department of Education. In another digest it is noted:

"Tutoring is probably the best way for parents to participate in public education, according to Rich.[79] Intensive, one-to-one teaching is highly effective, and, unlike meetings, it does not take parents away from their children and their home. Tutoring can be as simple as reading a book or discussing a television show. It may entail meeting with a teacher to determine how to help with homework. Or it can mean mastering a detailed curriculum written by specialists in home learning."

Bubba's neuropsychologist was familiar with the special education personnel at Bubba's school because he frequently evaluated children from the district as well as other districts. When I informed him about my intent to get "The Program" into Bubba's IEP, he stated that it would be difficult because "they don't want to set a precedent." In reality, he was probably right. If the district provided effective tutoring for one student, and other parents found out about it, then they would be asking for effective tutoring also!

Statistical Note on the Cost of Special Education

Students in special education cost more – The per pupil education spending for students receiving special education services are approximately two times greater than the spending on students who receive no special education. In the 1977-78 school year, the costs for special-education students averaged about $3,577 per child, compared to an average of $1,650 for those students not in special education. For the 1999-2000 school year, the average expenditure per pupil for students with disabilities (excluding homebound students) was $12,525. The average expenditure for regular education students was $6,556.[80]

---

[79] Dorothy Rich, "The Forgotten Factor in School Success: The Family; A Policymaker's Guide," District of Columbia: The Home and School Institute, 1985.

[80] Special Education Expenditure Project, "Total Expenditures for Students with Disabilities, 1999-2000: Spending Variation by Disability," June, 2003.

"Love of Music"

In Summary

More attention is now being paid to parental involvement as a fundamental element in the academic success of all children.[81]

I worked part-time while Bubba was in middle school and high school. I often got comments like, "That must leave you with a lot of spare time," or "Why don't you work full-time," or "What do you do with your time?"

To command a high hourly rate with clients that were forgiving about showing up late every Wednesday, leaving early every day, taking several days off to attend IEP and teacher meetings, along with other missed time for normal sickness and emergencies, I had to be very good at my job. Having twenty-plus years of experience, a bachelor's, two master's, a doctorate degree and professional networking didn't necessarily hurt either, but the primary factor in obtaining and maintaining employment was delivering client requests with a high degree of accuracy first, and with quick turnaround whenever possible. That approach allowed me to have so much "spare time" and the financial resources to provide tutoring and all the other special activities

---

[81] Arlene Sacks, *Special Education: A Reference Handbook* (Santa Barbara, California: ABC-CLIO Inc., 2001).

that were important for building Bubba's skills and confidence. My goal was to keep doors open for his future, provide guidance and allow him the opportunity to pursue his life independently.

Most of the characters that I encountered seemed to have a genuine interest in helping kids, but school district personnel are subject to certain constraints – time, money and the law. It seemed like the dollars flowing to effective remediation activities like one-on-one tutoring got overlooked and short-changed.

The special education system is just that – a system. While I was being specially educated, I recognized that I was dealing with a system that consisted of an ever-changing cast of characters operating with slices of Bubba's educational experience. There was no "system memory" in the sense that folks in one year remembered that a particular approach had already been tried and failed.

I had only one child to manage and could remember his education history perfectly, but unfortunately, that didn't count when team meetings revolved around methodology options for Bubba, because I was a parent and not an expert. One year's team wouldn't recognize that the services that were supposed to be provided by the previous year's team had not been provided. I remembered, but who wants to hear that sad song in a team meeting; and it was fruitless to try to get team members to look through prior year's logs and acknowledge that what was agreed upon, didn't occur. When I sensed that doors were closing for Bubba, my approach was to provide the service I felt he needed and take on the system retroactively.

And I put a lot of effort into getting compensated for the tutoring to remediate Bubba's reading, writing, math and confidence. Did I need the reimbursement money? Not really. I would have provided the same activities even if I wasn't reimbursed because they were necessary and appropriate.

As a taxpayer paying for special education, it was particularly disturbing to see very little special education occurring during the school day, while I was working a part-time schedule to not only pay for, but provide the services at home. As a taxpayer, paying for uninformed and misdirected activities by school district personnel that sometimes compounded Bubba's problems was even more disturbing. Reading hundreds of cases and browsing statistics that indicated that I was not alone was even more disturbing. There was no accuracy in their approach, and there certainly was no quick turnaround when it came to providing services or documentation to account for those services.

Operation Bury Them in Paperwork evolved over the course of several years as I collected the necessary documentation and generated charts to prove that tutoring was effective, necessary and appropriate for Bubba, and that the special education system was not providing it. While the term, "Bury Them" may sound a bit vindictive, burying the system was also necessary.

"Them" is a system composed of special education personnel who have a lot of paperwork to deal with in the normal course of operations. They have a lot of children to manage and have families and homes just like other people. The last thing they want to see is a notification of a complaint, a mediation request or a Due Process request when they are planning a nice trip for the summer, or planning a vacation and rest over winter break. And the last thing they want to see is another request when they just finished settling the previous request.

The alternative was to pay the taxes to support the special education and pay for (and provide much of) the special education out-of-pocket as well. And after paying for the education and then providing the education, I suppose I could "deal with it" as Bubba would say. I understood that even though it may not be fair, and I was angry and frustrated, going through the difficulties of getting retroactively reimbursed might not be worth the effort. And maybe it wasn't worth the effort, but I pursued that course anyway.

My sweet little angel began his public school career with a prognosis of never being able to read. This is not a prognosis filled with hope. That he would never be able to write. That he couldn't take a foreign language. That he wouldn't be an athlete. That college algebra would be too difficult. That he couldn't pass his graduation tests and the tests could be waived. That he couldn't learn cursive. That he shouldn't be in the regular classroom.

The prognosis was wrong.

Specially Educated

I picked Bubba up from the airport a few days ago. He spent the last half of his eighteenth year living in an apartment in Tel-Aviv, on his own, within the structure of a gap year program. He attended college (taking a foreign language) and was responsible for producing his own written work as part of the course requirements. He volunteered at the dog shelter and with the military. He was responsible for sharing duties at the apartment, doing cooking and laundry, as well as managing his finances, personal purchases and brushing his teeth. He managed to navigate his way though a foreign country, an international airport, back through the Philadelphia airport, and finally back home. I think he has been specially educated.

www.ingramcontent.com/pod-product-compliance
Lightning Source LLC
Chambersburg PA
CBHW041351290426
44108CB00001B/8